Lessons Learned at Ground Zero

Thank you for all you do for children and our country.

Robert Gillio MD   2006

As the soot and dirt and ash rained down,
We became one color.
As we carried each other down the stairs of the
burning building,
We became one class.
As we lit candles of waiting and hope,
We became one generation.
As the firefighters and police officers fought their
way into the inferno,
We became one gender.
As we fell to our knees in prayer for strength,
We became one faith.
As we whispered or shouted words of
encouragement,
We spoke one language.
As we gave our blood in lines a mile long,
We became one body.
As we mourned together the great loss,
We became one family.
As we cried tears of grief and loss,
We became one soul.
As we retell with pride of the sacrifice of heroes,
We become one people.

We are
One color
One class
One generation
One gender
One faith
One language
One body
One family
One soul
One people

We are The Power of One.
We are United.
We are America.

…Author Unknown

Lessons Learned at Ground Zero

Robert Gillio, MD
Edited by MaryAlice Bitts

Teacher's Choice Press

San Jose New York Lincoln Shanghai

Lessons Learned at Ground Zero

Teacher's Choice Press
an imprint of iUniverse, Inc.

For information address:
iUniverse, Inc.
5220 S. 16th St., Suite 200
Lincoln, NE 68512
www.iuniverse.com

ISBN: 0-595-24350-9

Printed in the United States of America

When the world changed forever that day, the meaning of family changed forever, as well.

People from more than eighty countries died when the twin towers of the World Trade Center collapsed. Instead of being divided by this horrible tragedy, the world pulled together as an expanded family.

This book is dedicated to my family, and to all the families affected by the tragedy of September 11, 2001.

Contents

PART III: The Freedom Generation

Foreword

It was a chaotic time in the early days after 9/11. I was fortunate to be able to organize a health screening and triage activity for the NYPD rescuers who were experiencing symptoms as a result of their work at Ground Zero. My regular work with the Living Heart Foundation helps communities by screening students for underlying problems of a nutritional, pulmonary or cardiovascular nature. When we got to New York, it became apparent that respiratory problems from the dust, fumes and smoke were the most noticeable findings in these World Trade Center rescuers. I spoke to Dr. Robert "Rob" Gillio, and he responded with enthusiasm, imagination and skill. Who would have ever thought that a prototype school smoking prevention program would become part of the infrastructure that facilitated our examination of over 1700 heroes?

Rob talks about heroes and angels. He asks for people to be called to action to take care of themselves, and to look out for their neighbors. He urges us all to create health records and to encourage baseline screening, where appropriate. Finally, he asks that we all look to do whatever we can for our families, schools, and communities to make a difference. He calls on us all to recognize those heroes we live with, and who are on call in our community utilities, hospitals, police, ambulance, and fire departments.

I saw, first-hand, the things that volunteers who are willing to work and become trained can accomplish. Through our foundation, over 200 people cared for those in New York. We dealt with a disaster that had never before been anticipated. We wrestled with economic, legal and political issues that were designed for ordinary situations, while we stepped into the extraordinary. The willingness to volunteer and take some risks made the difference.

Rob returned to Lancaster and pursued his vision for schools to be a center of a community network for education, health, and safety, in peacetime and in times of crises. He eventually was invited to the White House to discuss those views. I continued to encourage regular health evaluations for the surviving WTC heroes. The information we collected can be given to their doctors, who will determine if medical intervention is necessary. We do not yet know what the short- and long-term effects of the inhalation and traumatic exposure will be on these brave men and women.

At the time of this writing, it looks as if an optimistic course of action is developing. Mayor Bloomberg, Police Commissioner Kelly and dedicated members of the Columbia Presbyterian Medical campus in New York are working to establish a Columbia Stress Center so that well-meaning volunteers may never again need to fill that void. With Dr. Gillio's help, The Living Heart Foundation and its partner, The Edison Foundation, will assist with the analysis of the data we have collected and will ensure that the officers will continue to be seen by us, and be regularly examined by their personal doctors, for years to come. This will not only help to monitor their health, but will also help place each of them deservedly in the role of "hero" again, since the medical information they lend will guide the practitioners worldwide, who will then care for those thousands from over eighty countries exposed in the first days at Ground Zero.

Rob and I agree that our service at Ground Zero constituted the highlight of our professional lives. I hope you can find similar rewards in your communities. We are counting on you.

Dr. Arthur "Archie" Roberts
Founder of the Living Heart Foundation and Director of the
Ground Zero Clinic for the NYPD

Ackowledgements

There are so many people that I'd like to thank—so many who gave generously of their time, their knowledge, their hearts during this project—that I hesitate to begin, knowing that I will not be able to name them all. However, there are a few who deserve special mention here.

Dr. Arthur "Archie" Roberts, and his Living Heart Foundation volunteers, whose quick response and tireless work set the wheels in motion.

My former med school faculty advisors, former Mayo Clinic physicians Edward Rosenow, Paul Enright and Robert Hyatt, who readily lent their expertise when I—and the New York Police Department—needed it most.

Dr. Peter Yellowlees in Australia, and the New Zealand company he referred me to, Doctor Global, which offered first responders lifetime access to their medical records, in an effort to help us better diagnose and treat the New York rescuers at the Ground Zero site.

My staff at InnerLink, Inc.—especially top management Robert Walton, Martha Harris and Michael Curley—who supported my efforts at Ground Zero, and helped launch our company to new horizons following the September 11 attacks, and the many volunteers who left their homes, families and businesses in Lancaster, PA to help support the effort in New York City.

Chance Conner, whose expert editing of the first draft of this book was invaluable, and MaryAlice Bitts, who saw the book through to its final form and built the supporting web site.

My wife, Beth, both for her excellent work by my side at Ground Zero, and for her emotional and practical support, enabling me to go forth and complete my work, not only during this project, but throughout my career. My in-laws for taking care of our children while Beth was at Ground Zero with me, and my children for giving their blessing to the project, as well.

Finally, to the volunteers and heroes that support our local communities that give us the insight into what was sacrificed in New York.

Prologue

After September 11, 2001, we didn't need the media to tell us that something monumental had happened. As tragic as the events at the Pentagon, the crash in Western Pennsylvania and the World Trade Center complex were—and they most certainly were, especially to those who lost loved ones that day, or suffered damages to their health during the event, or in the aftermath—we all understood almost immediately that the impact of this day reached far beyond those losses. The world itself had changed forever.

We knew that we had to respond. But what should we do, in these new, uncertain times? What, in fact, *could* we do, as individuals, as families, as corporations, organizations, communities?

I was thinking about that question from my home in Lancaster, Pennsylvania at the time of the Attack on America, in the fall of 2001—the time that changed the way that Americans viewed themselves, and their world. I had just gotten InnerLink, Inc. (***www.innerlinkit.com***), my hands-on and Internet-based education company, off the ground, and together, with a talented team, I had created several products to help students work with real experts to solve real problems and, in the process, to learn about careers, science and the excitement of being part of a team that would accomplish something to benefit mankind.

We knew these were idealistic goals, but we also knew they were also entirely attainable. By the time the Towers collapsed, we had already devised an Outer Space project that had launched aboard the Space Shuttle, and that continues to help NASA scientists plan a food production system for deep space exploration. Our Project Breathe product was formed to create a high-quality interactive education experience, encouraging students to refuse to begin smoking, or to quit their habit, if they already have. In fact, it was this project that came to shape my work at Ground Zero, and it is this project that I continue to use in helping others to become safer, and better prepared for the unexpected.

I am explaining the nature of my work here, because it is central to my post-9/11 work in national emergency preparedness.

The concept is simple. In Project Breathe, students use virtual reality images of the body and expert content to learn about the lungs, how to prevent illness, how to screen for undiagnosed illness and how to build a medical record on paper, as well as online. The device also allows them to work with a team of world-class researchers and clinicians as mentors and as team leaders for research and screening activities. One of the highlights of the experience is the T.E.A.M. machine, an acronym based on its functions: Telecommunications, Education, Administration, and Measurement. This T.E.A.M. Machine is a laptop computer customized to allow for building an electronic health record and to do actual testing of the heart with electrocardiography, and the lungs with spirometry and pulse oxymetry measurements. It also can be used as a network communications device in times of emergency, allowing for communities, schools, local governments, fire departments, police departments and other organizations to quickly access information from key sources—and allowing diagnosticians access to medical records and reference materials while on site at a disaster scene. It also provides quick, on-site tutorials for volunteers—in emergencies, or in peacetime. It was this aspect of the program that was to become so vital to my post-9/11 work.

Connecting students and others with experts—and needed information—in times of peace and emergency is vital. In its "Project Breathe" mode, the machine allows students to be in touch daily with medical care providers in their community throughout the program's duration, as they learn about healthcare careers. If a disaster strikes, each of those settings immediately converts to become a site where care can be rendered under expert advice until advisors arrive. If the local medical experts are unreachable or overwhelmed, others on site can create a secondary support in a telemedical network of advisors. It also allows for on-site access to medical information, for aid with on-site diagnosis for healthcare professionals, as I was to demonstrate during my own work at Ground Zero.

When planes crashed into the Twin Towers, into the Pentagon, and into the ground in Western Pennsylvania on September 11, 2001, we all learned that these tools were much more valuable than any of us could ever have dreamed or wanted them to be. This is, however, a different world than it was on September 10 of that year, and while we must continue with our lives with hope for the future, we must also be safe and smart, and fully prepared for any event, should the extraordinary once again occur on these shores.

When I asked Pennsylvania Governor Mark Schweiker what we—as businesses and community leaders and citizens in the private sector—could do to help in these times of heightened security, he told me to encourage our employees and fellow community members to volunteer and support our efforts to better prepare our businesses, communities and organizations for the unexpected. He also asked that we inform our local and state emergency agencies of our skills, resources and capabilities.

My professional and personal goals are to help us all prepare to deal with disasters locally so that we can survive nationally. My company is dedicated to helping. Any income related to this activity will be invested 100 percent back into the effort to improve our ability to help.

I encourage corporate leaders to look at their intellectual property, products and personal services and see how they can support their communities. The return to the staff and business is much greater than profit.

I have therefore focused my own employees and advisors to identify world-class resources in telecommunications, education, administration, and measurement technology that can be bundled together in a coordinated way to help first responders and citizens. We have expanded our curriculum tools for schools and have invented a new way for schools, companies and homes to be linked to a central database, where there is shared information. We hope this online operations and disaster manual will be perpetually updated, will help with day-to-day efficiencies and will ease the response to a disaster. We worked to create services that have a triple use in high-quality, inquiry-based education that helps schools reach their standards. We hope to focus our towns, agencies and resources into an inner-linked community, because if we work together better in ordinary times, we will be better prepared when the extraordinary happens.

We have motivated our team to create a Citizen's Corp Council, a Community Emergency Response Team, a Medical Reserve Corps, Block Watches, and in-school curriculum to prepare our community for more effective preparations and communications during ordinary times/peacetime, so that we can all be ready for extraordinary times/ crisis. In order to get helpful information to the public as quickly as possible, we are committed to continually updating our web site (***www.innerlinkit.com/lessonslearned***) as information becomes available to us.

What can other individuals, families, communities, organizations, companies do to best prepare for the future in this post-9/11 era? The first step is to become as knowledgeable as possible. You have bought this book, and are about to learn about a doctor's experiences treating rescuers at the Ground Zero site, and what some recommended steps toward preparation might be. That's a good first step.

I hope by the end of the book, you are motivated to take your place in history and become part of the Freedom Generation in these difficult times. You will learn how to become part of the Freedom Generation, and begin to make a difference.

PART I

The Ground Zero Clinic

1

Surrounded by Heroes and Angels: An e-mail home from Ground Zero my first night

9/29/01 1:40 a.m.:

Dear Beth,

I can't sleep. I have seen things today that amaze me and challenge my ability to understand them. It is a day of contrasts and extremes. It is a grand adventure and a fascinating mission. But most importantly, it is a time for me to be among the angels and the heroes who are here.

The day begins at 5:30 a.m. I make my way past huge trucks that are blocking the entranceway to a secure street in the NYPD's 13th Precinct. There are American flags everywhere in Manhattan. But even with these visual reminders, it doesn't truly hit me that there is anything wrong until I enter the Police Academy Building. Then it gets much more real.

I initially notice a small memorial for Glenn, a videographer who was shooting tape for analysis of the terrorist crime scene when he was killed in the collapse of the towers. Inside the Academy, candles, pictures, wreaths and cards are everywhere. Near the elevator, beyond another checkpoint and inside the building, I see more reminders of where I am. Xeroxed papers with the words "missing but not forgotten" are affixed to the walls. A poster with pictures of thirteen lost police officers, draped with the green and blue colors of the NYPD, is in full view. Ribbons of the same colors are on everyone's nametags.

The building is a mess. A huge gymnasium has been transformed into a dormitory, complete with piles of towels and underwear, bare cots—no sheets or pillows are on them—and a table of food in huge, plastic, thermos-like trays from the Red Cross. The trash cans have not been emptied. In what is usually a regimented, paramilitary drilling area, there is a television quietly tuned to CNN. Throughout the building, people try to nap.

We begin to prepare the makeshift clinic. We are given a room that is used to train the SWAT team. We have no exam tables. We move tables and desks, and put the workout mats on them. One officer, who had worked beneath the collapsing buildings and survived, now finds himself tumbling off our exam table when a mat unexpectedly shifts. Another table has a broken leg, so we scrounge around this run-down 1940's fortress for sturdier furniture. (We find some duct tape and manage the best we can.)

The volunteers here are from Las Vegas, Portland and from just around the corner, on 23rd Street. There is a sense of adventure and apprehension as we await the officers who have learned of the opportunity to get their lungs checked. We don't know how many to expect. We had planned on using certain equipment but it didn't arrive, so we use our laptop computers, and then go out to a store to buy a printer. Despite the décor, we are safe and comfortable.

I worry that I will be hit with a wave of emotions and will have trouble keeping my composure when I start to interact with these officers—much as I did on September 11, when I thought about how we would tell our children that their innocent world had been forever changed...

I wrote that email on my first night at Ground Zero when I, and a small corps of volunteers, forfeited a few days with our families to help determine the health effects that many police and rescue teams had experienced, as a result of the toxins they had been exposed to at Ground Zero.

Our job was to give the rescue and security workers an opportunity to get a medical checkup without having to worry about the impact the results might have on their jobs. The workers had been consistently told that they faced no health risks, but they read in the newspapers, and saw on television, that the air quality at Ground Zero was dangerous. One of the officers assigned to the Office of Emergency Management (OEM) wasn't shy about reporting that the city and the state had conducted a series of tests, and had said that the air was safe. Later, federal authorities came in with great fanfare, and created alarm by declaring it a contaminated area, where the use of respirators was now an absolute requirement.

The politics of inter-departmental issues, disability, workman's compensation and liability weighed heavily on the minds of city administrators and the unions that represented the workers. Men and women who had lost friends, relatives and colleagues—and who had put their own lives on the line—were exhausted and apprehensive. They also, of course, worried about their health. For the next four days, I heard the same questions: "Am I going to be all right, doc?" and "Did the tests show that there is no damage or risk for the future?"

And although I saw no signs of hate or anger, I did see a deep concern over the lack of preparedness for the next possible terrorist event.

Despite these many fears, the rescue workers were appreciative of the volunteers. The heroes referred to the volunteers as "angels" and the volunteers reciprocated, calling them the same.

The first volunteer I met was a cardiology technician who was there to do echocardiograms and ECGs. He was shy about telling me his first name, explaining, "It is not a good name to have these days." I noticed he worked harder than anyone that first day, and that he did his job without ceremony, then quietly left. I never got a chance to thank him for his help. Later, I learned why he was reluctant to divulge his identity; his name was Osama.

One by one, I interviewed, examined and conducted heart and breathing tests on officers who were there when "It" happened on September 11. They didn't say much about the attacks until they were asked about them; then they answered in ways that reminded me of my father when I asked him about his experience on Iwo Jima during World War II, speaking in somber tones, and offering brief, unembellished answers. The members of our team explained to them that it was necessary to document their degree of exposure in order to study the effects and to help make medical decisions. We told them that what we learned about the risks of their exposure could help scientists and doctors advise the general public and their colleagues who experienced less exposure from the Twin Towers collapse.

They remained polite and courteous. In a "just the facts" manner, with little emotion, they told us their respective locations and the things they experienced or observed on September 11. While we had all turned to television or rushed home from work when the news of the attacks on the Twin Towers and in Washington broke, they had gone to the World Trade Center as fast as they could to help.

I met a man who told me that a person standing next to him died instantly when a body fell on them from one of the WTC towers. Two officers told me they were trapped for hours inside the remains of their car. Many were enveloped in dust and debris after looking up and realizing that the towers were falling. These were the people that the world saw covered in dust on that horrible day. These were the heroes who, when the dust settled, realized that dozens of their friends and thousands of their fellow citizens were inside those collapsed buildings. These were the men and women who stayed and dug and assisted, working double shifts for the next eighteen days. Their stories are fascinating, but the quiet and calm manner in which they conveyed them to our corps of volunteers was extremely eerie.

They were so appreciative of us and wondered why we went to the trouble of coming to New York to check them out. We were amazed that no one had come sooner. After all, it had been three weeks since the attacks. Medical science had not seen a situation like this before, and now the world was at risk for it to occur again—and possibly again and again. We needed to figure out how to best care for these heroes. If we were to be prepared for the ensuing personal and public health medical treatment issues, we needed to learn what the effects from the inhalation of a multitude of toxins would be.

The officers were gripped by a fear that they would not find their friends, and that the families of the victims would not be able to find a semblance of closure on it all. We also met some officers who were not allowed to search, but were instead assigned to other necessary jobs elsewhere in the city. They hadn't even seen Ground Zero. Some of them complained of insomnia and chest pains. In some ways, they experienced a the kind of tortured feelings that some of us who were far from Ground Zero felt, when we wished that we could do something to help.

I met cadets who had only just started the introductory weeks of their New York Police Academy training when "It" happened. They had been assigned police officer tasks, working the streets and "securing buildings and checkpoints"—without guns or vests—while their colleagues went into disaster mode. I met police officers from Deerfield, Illinois and Toledo, Ohio, who came to Manhattan on their vacation time, to help fill in for the NYPD officers.

Each and every one of these men and women were gracious to us, and they thanked us for caring for them. They treated us like heroes, as we sat in relative comfort in the Police Academy SWAT team training room. While we worked, food was delivered, along with notes of thanks. Some gave us an NYPD patch, a ball cap or a shirt as a way to thank us for caring.

When we pointed out the obvious paradox—that we had come to take care of them, while they cared for us, in return—we were told by some that they had never, in their careers, felt cared for by others. "We are givers, not takers," said one officer. "We are really a little bit meek and shy when someone shows us any courtesy. It just rarely happens, and we are grateful but uncomfortable in this role." Another officer, with tears in his eyes, said, "One thing is for sure: Those letters and pictures from kids across the country kept us going."

I believe their acknowledgement of our presence there represented their need to say "thank you" to the people they will never meet personally—those who sent food, clothing, cards and donated blood. I vowed to myself that I would push to encourage people all throughout the country to stop and thank the police and fire departments in their communities for being there, twenty-four hours a day, seven days a week. I thought of the water and the power and the communications workers, who brought back lights, water and phone service after the attacks. I wondered if anyone ever thanked them for being on call and working in dangerous situations after storms, fires and other disasters, and I thought of ways that the technology my company employs could help those departments in case something happens in their towns.

The officers didn't realize it, but the team of doctors there—and others across the country—really didn't know the exact effects of the contaminants on their systems. We discussed among ourselves the possible triggering agents of asthma, alveolar proteinosis, hypersensitivity pneumonitis, asbestosis and mesothelioma. We queried each other about previous studies regarding the effects of dust arising from ruins filled with the organic material that was once human beings. We called upon our colleagues at Mayo and Hopkins for help. We held meetings. We talked about science, but also politics, so that we could design a study that could be made without jeopardizing the department or the unions. We set a deadline for forty-eight hours to have a proposal ready.

We were working in an environment in which the acute phase of the illnesses that some of the officers had experienced had passed, due to delays. We didn't have good information on the air quality or dust analysis. Our specific inquiries led to an invitation, days later, to join the representatives of the Centers for Disease Control (CDC), the National Institutes on Occupational Safety and Health (NIOSH), New York State Department of Health, New York City Department of Health, and other doctors and epidemiologists in a series of conference calls, where I share our clinical observations and concerns.

We faced many logistical challenges. We realized that we didn't have access to previous records for a department that lost its operational headquarters in the WTC, and then we found that its phone lines were nearly useless in its main headquarters. We found abnormalities in many officers, but without previous records to compare the results with, we didn't know if the conditions were acute or chronic. (I filed this away as something that could easily be solved with an electronic medical record with Smart card technology backup.)

2

Sight, Sound and Smell: Introducing "The Pile"

Another doctor and I elected to go to Ground Zero to see for ourselves just how severe the exposures were. We did not have passes to get into the Red Zone at the WTC, but we knew that we needed to get there to understand what problems we were trying to solve. (We were also very curious and a bit voyeuristic, but we hesitated to articulate that fact to each other.)

The security was intense. We needed to cross nine checkpoints to get there, after walking two miles from a point where no cars had access. We flashed our borrowed access passes, and explained our interest as lung experts to a phalanx of officers as we advanced closer. We passed a mass of people waving signs to the rescue and recovery vehicles, and shouting, "Thank you" to the nation's heroes.

From a distance I could see that there was some construction equipment. We entered a massive beehive of activity with construction vehicles and armed guards in military attire. We passed barricades, dump trucks and bulldozers. When we were still four blocks away, they confiscated my backpack and camera. (I was told that this was because no photographs were permitted, out of respect for grieving families, but I later learned that authorities had been warned that foreign agents may have used photos to analyze the way the response was conducted, which could have helped with additional attacks or aided the design of other terrorist activities.) Just past the next checkpoint, I saw the school where our clinic was originally to be housed, IU89. If there had been mass casualties, this would have been a perfect triage or treatment center. Chills rolled up my back and down my arms when I thought about the White Paper I first drafted more than a year ago which detailed the use of schools as emergency health facilities.

A colorful collection of bright yellow, pink, red and orange tents, trailers and vehicles were everywhere. Command posts for the OEM, Red Cross, Secret Service and dozens of other organizations were there. Workers from companies such as Verizon hustled about. There were many steel workers, and men and women working sixteen cranes spanned across my line of sight. We looked around in utter amazement. I imagined that a similar bustle of activity took place when this structure was built. We could smell raw sewage and nearly fell into a manhole as we walked along, mesmerized by the scene.

In an email to my wife, Beth, I described what it was like behind the barricades at Ground Zero that day:

...Some call it "The Pile." Others call it "The Pit." It is the debris that was once three buildings in the WTC complex. It covers four square blocks, but follows the street grid in an orderly chaos of steel and cement and dust. There is dust everywhere. Over the last 18 days, workers have eradicated mountains of it from the area, but every wisp of wind and activity from the recovery effort raises more of it.

The Pile is like several heaps of Lincoln Logs, only these "logs" are twisted metal surrounded by cement and dust. Nonetheless, they are stacked one over another, as if a monstrous trash compactor had simply tried to push the buildings into the ground.

We are viewing the side that is the remains of Building Seven. It has been reduced to a height of seven stories. On it are three gigantic cranes, large enough to pick up a Volkswagen with one bite. They resemble robotic dinosaurs devouring a huge carcass. Two sit atop The Pile and are precariously balanced, grabbing debris and throwing it to the ground below. I wonder how they got up there. It seems horrific to think that the cranes are moving so aggressively when there may be survivors or even bodies beneath them.

On a subsequent visit to the NYPD headquarters as an official guest later that afternoon, I learned that this building collapsed six hours after the others and was fully evacuated.

Around it were men in cages, dangling fifteen stories above the ground in huge cranes, and cutting steel on buildings across the street. We looked up and realized that hundreds of partially broken windows were above us, and that they could fall on us—or on the workers—at any time. They had not yet been boarded up, a full eighteen days after the blast. There was too much else to do on the ground. We were not as brave as we thought we were; we moved on quickly to be out of harm's way. The others stayed behind, continuing their work.

As we rounded another corner, the dust and the odor hit us full in the face. We were wearing our masks, but felt silly because most of the hundreds of fatigued workers simply had them hanging around their necks.

Then we saw that familiar scene—the scene of jumbled, skeletal architectural remains of buildings that we've come to know from the images we've seen on television. It somehow seemed both well-known and detached from us, perhaps because we had seen this image filtered through the media so many times, it somehow didn't seem quite real. Even though we were right there, near the workers, it was as though we were a long distance away from them. I wished I had my binoculars, so I could see them better.

The recognizable façade still stood and I remembered walking through those doors with Mike Curley, my colleague at InnerLink, when we visited New York just a few months before, for a meeting. We had wanted to go to the top to see the view, but the $18 price tag—and the prospect of waiting in line with dozens of tourists—hadn't seemed worth it at the time. I wondered aloud if there was a line to go to the top of the towers on the morning of the attacks.

At The Pile, my senses were overwhelmed. What I saw was far worse than I had anticipated—far worse than what I had seen on TV. The scale was immense, filling my visual field with the devastation all around me. The air held an odor that reminded me of my childhood. I realized that it reminded me of the scent I had smelled when the motor on my Lionel train had burned out. I hadn't thought about that train for years. There were also occasional whiffs of decay, the smell of death. The smell was subtle—not dramatic or overpowering—but it was there.

The noise was loud and continuous. My ears were assaulted by the sounds of construction equipment gnawing at The Pile: steel cutting, saws slicing through beams, the morgue refrigerator trailer compressors, hundreds of vehicles and occasional voices. It was not the still, silent memorial- or cemetery-like atmosphere I had expected.

The biggest surprise, however, was the distinctive, chalky taste of drywall dust in my mouth. The air itself was dusty, and it instantly made my nose and mouth dry. My eyes watered. I thought that if the air left a residue to taste in the mouth, the dust must have also been getting in my eyes and lungs. I looked around and saw the same moist eyes in the volunteers from the Red Cross and from the tough, rugged construction and rescue workers. I wondered if perhaps this was a result of chemical and particulate irritation.

My own tears, I knew, were caused not only environmental irritants; my emotions were trying to rise to the surface. As I moved through the site, I knew I had to work to keep these emotions in check.

As I continued walking, I saw a striking technique employed by the workers. Using trolls and spades, they gently sifted through the pile, looking for remains. Then a crane took it down a bit lower, as it gently removed one piece of steel at a time. Men and women with acetylene torches cut steel to help with its removal. I later learned during a working group conference call that an analysis of the CDC's personal contamination monitors showed very high levels of carbon monoxide in these workers. That news made monitoring for heart disease an even bigger priority.

The workers were hit with a plume of dust that billowed high into the sky. There was a hint of smoke, but I assumed that it was only dust.

I later learned that a fire still burned deep inside the pile. The steel is hot and the organic debris smoldered, leaping to flame once oxygen was allowed in. It was reminiscent of the fires in the ground near Centralia, Pennsylvania that have burned for years in an old coal mine.

These brave workers were performing a difficult and thankless job. There were no more bucket brigades in view. There was nothing to find. Everything was pulverized or vaporized. We saw no desks or chairs, rugs or curtains. We saw no bodies. We were watching the cremation of the remains of thousands of people. We felt and smelled the presence of death.

The officers used search-and-rescue dogs in vain, and some of these animals had been cut and injured. Some were dehydrated, and I was told that two dogs had died.

We also saw what was called a "cadaver dog," a highly skilled animal that was trained to find dead bodies based on a foul, distinctive odor. It was clear that the dog was excited, but couldn't settle on one location, perhaps because so many bodies did not survive the long, hideous fall intact. We learned that many of the dogs were despondent, because they had been trained to find and rescue live people in wreckage at disaster sites, but had instead found so many corpses and remains. Some volunteers had actually hidden in the rubble, in order to lift the spirits of these animals—giving the dogs an opportunity to "rescue" a live human, and enabling them to continue working.

As we walked through The Pile, witnessing all of these extraordinary sights, we were simply fascinated observers. Then, as I began to think of the braveness and heroism that surrounded me, amid all the construction site noise and activity, it suddenly seemed to me to be strangely quiet, as if these noises were, instead, angels humming a hymn. Then the doctor part of me suppressed that emotional side of the experience for the moment. It would not have helped to let that side go free, even though internally, I realized I was surrounded by heroes and angels.

Except for the flags and the traffic, I was struck by just how normal the city seemed only a fifteen-minute walk from Ground Zero. I wondered what Gettysburg, Berlin, Pearl Harbor, Hiroshima, Seoul or Saigon looked like in the weeks and months after their infamous attacks. I developed a deeper appreciation for the challenges that previous generations had faced, and the things that they had feared. We had all endured a horrible day and it has affected us all. I hoped we would not have a series of days or years like this ahead of us.

We headed back to the clinic to do several more hours of screenings. We had smelled the odors, breathed the smoke and coughed the dust in our throats. This was all on the eighteenth day following September 11; the conditions earlier after the attack must have been unlike anything I have ever seen, medically speaking. We realized we had to get our hands on the sophisticated data analysis that someone must have done on the exposures.

It took us five hours before we finally got access to some data—but only by working our way up the tedious chain of command at NIOSH. There was no coordinated effort to share the information already gathered, and wild and unfounded rumors abounded. I was determined to get the best minds in the country involved in our effort. I made calls that led to a meeting with the leadership of the American Association of Respiratory Care, American College of Chest Physicians and the National Lung Health Education Program.

Back at the clinic, I described the end of my day to my wife in an email home:

I am exhausted and, as I move the medical equipment out of the way, lay out the mats the SWAT team uses to practice takedowns, I try to get some sleep. I think about my first day as a volunteer. I am nervous that our help won't be needed and I will suddenly feel silly. I struggle with my ignorance about inhalation injury as I plan a meeting to design a study with the experts involved. I spent three hours in hell at Ground Zero. We have seen more than 70 people today, each with a horrific experience as bad as the next. Each one is mourning the loss of one or more friends. The housing is a haphazard arrangement of cots, with people sleeping in the locker room, gymnasium and in our modified clinic. Some of our staff goes to hotels on their companies' expense accounts; others go home to New Jersey.

Honey, I choose to sleep here to watch over the equipment and clean up after everyone leaves. I am glad I did. There is camaraderie among all of us during those rare evenings when things slowed down. I was an outsider but was treated like a brother. I enjoy this part of the experience more than anything I have done in a long time. I try to sleep. I am interrupted by three different officers who come up to make sure I have a blanket or something to eat. One officer lingers until after midnight and shares his story, asking for my advice and counsel. How do you tell a man who has lost his partner, and has been working every waking hour for days at The Pile, that you are tired and want to sleep?

I learn about how he lost consciousness for an indefinite period of time after the first tower nearly fell on him. Immediately enveloped in dust, he remembers taking two breaths, then being unable to breathe, but still passing out. He still coughs up muddy-looking material. He is concerned for his health, his job, his emotional condition and his family. Our visit lasted until 1:00 a.m. We conducted a visit that no doctor or patient could ever have had in today's medical machine system. We are both grateful for the visit.

I meet people who witnessed the collapse of the first tower, and emerged from the dust. Rather than lick their wounds and retreat to safety, they ran into the second tower, knowing a collapse was imminent. They are surprised at my amazement, saying that it is all part of the job. During the course of my career I have met astronauts, governors, famous actors and even a king. I have never, ever met more impressive people than I have met today...

I maintained my composure and professionalism throughout the day. In many ways the day was filled with fascination as well as denial. The combination of that fascination and emotion was very much like what I felt while waiting for one of our babies to be born. I remember as I "helped" in the delivery room, I denied the risks and maintained my focus, so that my emotions wouldn't distract anyone else. The process fascinated me. Then, once I realized what had just happened, the emotions washed down over me.

I try to sleep with my eyes closed, but the stories and the images of the day won't go away. I recall a brief phone conversation I had during a break in the action at the clinic. It was a call home to wish Maria a happy 8th birthday. Then the phone was handed to one of her sisters, who asked, "Did you actually see it?" She was referring to the devastation at the site of the former World Trade Center. I told her that I had. Her voice got real quiet and she said in the same slow, somber tone—the same tone I've been hearing all day: "Then I guess that's it. That's it. That means it really happened. I was hoping you would say it wasn't true and that this was all a big, cruel lie" As I think back on her words and especially the way she said them, that is when my fascination ends and my emotions hit home.

Give the kids a big hug for me. I promise to stay safe. Thanks for allowing me to leave everything to you at home while I enjoy the privilege of living here with the angels and heroes.

Love always,

Rob

3

How did I get here? Some Background Information

I was sitting with my wife, Beth, in our home in Lancaster, Pennsylvania, when I saw the World Trade Center leveled, live, on television. I am a physician trained in pulmonary and intensive care unit medicine, and we knew that there would be an overwhelming need for doctors to help treat the massive casualties. As the day unfolded and planes hit the Pentagon and crashed in western Pennsylvania—possibly en route to our local nuclear power plant, Three Mile Island—it became increasingly clear that the country and the world were facing unprecedented challenges. I called and volunteered to help with the Red Cross and the Pennsylvania Medical Society.

No one called during the next two weeks. People either survived without much injury or died, as innocent victims or as heroic rescuers. I was saddened by all of the fatalities, but relieved that I didn't need to leave my family to face the uncertainty of working in a war zone. My greatest fear was that anthrax would be found in the dust of the World Trade Center, as part of the terrorism attack, because I knew that by the time anthrax would be discovered among the carnage, thousands would be infected. I also knew that we were ill-prepared as a nation to deal with a bioterrorism threat or attack. Although I am a lung specialist trained at Mayo Clinic, who has practiced for twenty years, I had never seen or heard a presentation on an anthrax case, and felt ill-prepared to handle such a case.

Since I knew no way to help, I settled down to trying to get Inner-Link, Inc. (***www.innerlinkit.com***), my hands-on and Internet-based education company, off the ground. We had risked everything financially to make this company a reality and had just closed on the funding for it to launch in earnest on September 9, 2001. One project my company was in the process of developing was to have a surprising connection to my work at Ground Zero, although we didn't know that at the outset.

That was our InnerSpace, our health education project, which we call Project Breathe. When Project Breathe was created, of course, we didn't know that terrorists would attack the World Trade Center and the Pentagon, or send another plane that would crash in Western Pennsylvania. The goal of Project Breathe to create an interactive education experience, encouraging students to refuse to begin smoking, or to quit if they already have. Using virtual reality images, students learn about the lungs, how to prevent illness, how to screen for undiagnosed illness and how to build a medical record on paper, as well as online. One of the highlights of the experience is the T.E.A.M. machine, and it was this aspect of the program that was to become so vital to my post-9/11 work. The T.E.A.M. device is an acronym based on its functions: Telecommunications, Education, Administration, and Measurement. It is a laptop computer customized to allow for building an electronic health record and to do actual testing of the heart with electrocardiography and the lungs with spirometry and pulse oxymetry measurements.

It was this function of the machine that I thought of when I received a call from Dr. Archie Roberts on September 28, 2000—a call that would lead to my work at the Ground Zero site. Archie is a retired cardiothoracic surgeon whose Living Heart Foundation had set up a program to help the Ground Zero rescuers. He had learned that the police officers of the NYPD were starting to develop symptoms of chest tightness and cough. There was no mechanism in place to determine who had critical levels of exposure and who had been, or was being, injured in the rescue effort. When the buildings fell, thousands of humans, computers, insulation and other materials were pulverized, vaporized and then burned. This meant that dust and debris was thick in the air, and the rescuers were breathing that air. The respiratory exposures were unprecedented, and a management team needed to be organized to determine the health of the rescuers at the scene.

There was also a need to determine the effects of the contaminants on the health of the thousands of lower Manhattan workers who also breathed potentially contaminated air.

Like many others in the country, I felt impotent, frustrated and unable to help in this time of need, so I was glad to learn of a way to help. The nation gave blood and sent money, but somehow, this does not feel as fulfilling as many of us wish. It was also obvious that anthrax had not been spread in the cloud of smoke and dust we all saw on TV.

My family gave their blessing for me to go. I asked Archie when I was needed in Lower Manhattan. "In twelve hours," came his reply.

How do you prepare for work at or near Ground Zero? I sure didn't know. This was uncharted territory for me. I simply grabbed some clothes, the T.E.A.M. machine, some spare clinical instruments and my CEO's laptop. Within three hours, I left my home to catch a train to New York City.

4

The Ground Zero Clinic

Once in New York, we set up camp. We took a school/administrative building and changed a portion of it into a dormitory and a field hospital screening clinic. This plan was reminiscent of a White Paper I'd written, which recommended using schools in this way, in times of crisis. (A copy of that White Paper, and other documents mentioned in this book, is on the InnerLink web site, *http://www.innerlinkit.com/lessonslearned.*)

The facility was in a disaster mode. The NYPD headquarters had relocated there after the emergency command center in the World Trade Center was destroyed and the phone lines leading to the downtown headquarters were cut in the disaster.

Every available officer was, in some way, fighting for the lives of the victims who might still be alive. For some, this meant literally searching for survivors; others secured a perimeter and guarded potential targets, like the city water supply and Grand Central Station. Detectives were assigned to the landfill, where they sifted through dust and debris for flight-data recorders, evidence and human remains.

The Police Academy building was filled with staff and volunteers who did not usually work there. Its gymnasium initially served as a triage and staging center after the buildings came down.

On the first day, the gymnasium overflowed with people who spontaneously showed up, seeking care for eye injuries and irritations. Now, it was a dormitory and food center. The Red Cross offered blankets and food. All day and night, people came and went, trying to get a few hours of rest. I tried to sleep there the first night, but found the constant interruptions intolerable. I eventually went up to the site of our clinic and slept on the floor.

Throughout the building, every quiet spot was filled by an officer or volunteer, covered with a Red Cross blanket, trying to sleep. No one complained. They all asked if I was OK—if I needed a blanket, or if I wanted food. When morning came, clean and new underwear, socks, and toiletries, were brought to us by volunteers. Notes and pictures of encouragement hung on the walls. I was tired, but these notes, and the strength of those around me, provided inspiration. I felt proud to be there, despite the fact that I had done very little, compared to the men and women who treated me as part of their team.

I went to Ground Zero several times. I was in the command center and saw the mother and wife of an officer being shown pins on a map, indicating the place where the officer was last known to be. They were told that the search-and-rescue effort to find the officer had become a search-and-recovery mission, because all hope of survival had passed. I heard their cries and saw their tears.

When I was in the Ground Zero morgue, I saw the procedure the workers followed when a body was found, or a when bucket with human remains arrived. I was there to observe the inadequate use of masks and of proper universal precautions against infectious disease. I saw a firefighter's body recovered and realized that the only way he could be identified was by the remnants of his uniform. I saw a collar bone and muscle on the body of a police officer, with a scorched portion of his bulletproof vest still attached. The body was logged in and placed on a stretcher in a tent, where a priest administered Last Rites. It was then transferred to the next tent, where a brief exam revealed the police clothing. The next stop was to a refrigerator trailer, and then off to the official morgue, where DNA analysis would determine his identity.

As I faced the grim realities of mortality, I thought about my late father, and his stories from another war. When the battle was over, the decaying remains of the soldiers from both sides of the Battle of Iwo Jima were scattered along the beaches. He had been assigned to the detail of collecting bodies and moving them to mass graves. Beyond recognition, American and Japanese were buried together. The battles of my father's generation lasted years and were scattered around the world, but in the end, they created an America that permitted me to live a life in freedom where I could pursue my dreams. My four daughters can aspire to any occupation they desire; they can vote and make choices that allow them to control their own lives. The horrors faced by the veterans of lengthy conflicts like the World Wars seemed overwhelming when I considered the destruction of the Twin Towers—which was, when viewed in this perspective, just one battlefield created from one attack.

As I left the morgue, I came across an officer who was trying to attach a large American flag to a railing. He asked if I could help. I had just seen the family of a victim receive devastating news of their loved one's loss, and had assessed the risks of future potential victims who were breathing all kinds of toxins. I had just seen a portion of a body—once an officer—placed in a bag and put into a refrigerator. As I held the flag, while duct tape was used to attach it to the railing, I found myself with tears in my eyes, standing straight and tall. I was honored to be helping with that flag at that place at that time, and I experienced a sense of patriotism as I had never felt before. I was proud to be an American. Again, I thought about my father and his service as a veteran, and as a patriotic citizen, and I felt privileged to be his son.

5

Asking the Right Questions

At the clinic, each day saw more and more officers seeking medical checkups. During the first days, we admitted about seventy people. By the end of our stay in New York, we had seen nearly 1,800 officers in three weeks. The staff that volunteered did not always have the appropriate skills to perform these tests—an ECG technician had cross-trained to do a spirometry, a spirometry technician had cross-trained to do ECG's—but we used our equipment to train them for quick, on-site in-service. Every day in the clinic was challenging, and it was busy.

The results we found caused us concern. Abnormalities in breathing tests and cardiac profiles were much higher than expected, and we struggled with finding the best ways to get these officers the appropriate follow-up care.

In order to understand and document the health risks the officers had experienced, we needed to question the officers thoroughly. We later learned that the form we put together for this purpose didn't capture all the data we would soon wish we had. When it got busy, we relied on the officers to fill out the form on their own, but on returning home, we discovered that when no volunteer was present to ask questions, the officers sometimes left some of the answers blank, or were inconsistent in their replies.

During that questioning, however, the facts that emerged, and the stories that were told, dramatically illustrated the exposures that these men and women endured: Were they there for the first Tower collapse, the second, or both? Did they arrive in the first hours after the collapse,

31

later that day, or on subsequent days? Did they work on The Pile or secure the perimeter a few blocks away? Did they have a mask and if so, what type? How did it fit, and did they actually wear it? Are they experiencing symptoms now? If so, how bad are they, and when did they begin? Are they getting treatment for their problems? Do their supervisors know about any problems they may be experiencing? What previous health problems do they have? Have they ever had a breathing test before so we may compare results?

Approximately one-third of the officers we talked to were there when the building crashed to the ground. They had received calls for all available officers to assist in the fire in the World Trade Center when the first plane hit. Many saw it fall first-hand, from a distance. Others ran for their lives. Others told of friends who lost their lives. In the building where we were holding the tests, they all knew Glenn, the videographer who was there to tape the scene for future training. A now-macabre graphic, created a month earlier and mounted on a door of the department, showed Glenn, a camera on his shoulder, with the World Trade Towers in the viewfinder.

6

Accounts of 9/11: The Heroes Speak

I pledged to the officers that our team would maintain their privacy. Therefore, I am not disclosing the names of any officer, nor am I telling their stories in full. Having conducted 1,800 interviews, however, I feel confident that I can relate a few brief sketches that illustrate the kinds of stories we heard and what exposure those police officers had, without divulging any specific details that would in any way reveal the identities of these brave men and women, and so, without breaking that trust.

As I spoke with more and more first responders, I learned that they all had common threads woven through them, but each was singularly gripping in its portrayal of true human courage and heroism in the face of chaos and terror.

An officer told us that he was at the site of the fire at the first tower. He and a partner saw debris fall, then herded people away from the base of the two towers. They ran under a walkway and to a garage, across the street. Some ran up the stairs into the building; others ran down into the garage as the building fell. When the plume of dust and debris came their way, the officers closed the garage door. It became pitch black in the structure, and the noise was thunderous. Five minutes later, when they opened the door, they could barely see, and began to cough. When they looked to the area where the others had run, they saw that the others that had been with them—those who had run the other direction—were all dead.

Another officer looked up, saw the tower falling, and dived under a walkway. He was pelted by bouncing debris, and covered his head. Because he was buried in dust, he had difficulty breathing. He lay in the prone position, certain that he was going to die. It was completely dark. He stood up, to try to get better air. He was convinced that the building had somehow collapsed around him, and that he was in a cave-like enclosure inside. For five minutes he waited to be rescued, breathing the thick, dusty air. He then sensed a bit of light and walked toward it, tripping on debris along the way.

After about a hundred yards it occurred to him that he was outside, and that the air was simply so thick with particulates that the light was not getting through. Rather than calling in sick or injured, he immediately began to look for survivors.

By the time I spoke with this officer, he had been working in the rescue effort for eighteen days of double shifts, and had not yet been home. He had had friends who were just a few feet away from him when he dived into the walkway for protection. Those friends had not yet been found, and were trapped beneath forty feet of rubble somewhere. He had a cough that was mildly productive, as well as gastrointestinal reflux symptoms. He had neither sought care, nor had he told his supervisors of his condition. Like many others, he had used his shirt or other pieces of cloth as a mask. Later, painter's masks arrived from Home Depot. (It wasn't until the fourth day that many rescuers received masks from the authorities, but most of those didn't fit properly. The appropriate double-filter respirator masks helped filter particulates and fumes, but made it hard for rescuers to communicate to each other during rescue work. Many had the attitude that they had already experienced a huge exposure and that the department was only now providing masks—and mandating their use—to avoid potential liability.)

Another officer was assisting an injured woman when the first building began to collapse. He grabbed her and ran into the doorway of an adjacent building. The force of the collapse created a wind tunnel that knocked them both down and almost immediately enveloped them in a dust cloud—a cloud so thick that the officer reported tasting and swallowing the dust in the air. He also reported the intense darkness that the dust and debris created on that otherwise clear September morning.

It was about this time that he noticed that the woman was not breathing. He realized her face was covered with debris and dust, and he used his hand to reach into her mouth to clear it. He used his own saliva and a mouth-to-mouth resuscitation effort to clear her nose and throat. When she began to breathe, he learned she was asthmatic, so he covered her head under his shirt in an attempt to minimize further exposure. After about five or ten minutes it became light and they ventured out, and he eventually handed her off to a rescue worker.

He told us he wandered around in a daze, helping where he could, when the second tower began to fall. He said that he felt the ground shake and instinctively looked up. He did not hear any warnings yet. He looked up and saw the now-familiar brown cloud above him approaching. He remembered yelling, "Go! Go! GO!!!" but not being able to move. Finally, with a second or two to spare, he ran and dived through a glass window in a nearby storefront. The force knocked him to the floor and covered him with glass. He got up out of the thick dust. Seconds later he was knocked to the floor again, when the dust cloud worked its way into the building from a stairwell and blasted him in another direction. After taking a few stitches, he was back at Ground Zero. He had tears in his eyes when he told us that no one had seen the woman or the rescuer from the first blast.

One cadet told me that he and a group of other cadets and officers were walking home from an off-duty security job and were just a few blocks away from the WTC when the first tower fell. Wanting to help, the small group rushed in the direction of the impact. He described the surrounding streets as a wasteland—like a lunar landscape—covered in dust, and devoid of any movement, light or sound. Dirt and dust were thick in the air, and shattered glass from blown-out storefront windows and other debris were strewn all about. The matter was thick in their throats and in their eyes, and the sky was dark. It was difficult to breathe and see, and their throats were scratchy and dry.

Out of this quiet desolation, the cadet heard an eerie hissing sound coming from a gourmet coffee shop. Amazed and curious, he made his way toward the noise and discovered its source: the shop's cappuccino machine was running! Still in shock, the cadet walked over to the machine, and started making lattes for the rest of the crew. The officers and cadets drank them quickly, their throats no longer dry. They organized a brief plan of action and moved out towards the remaining tower of the WTC to help evacuate it.

I never learned whether the other officers survived the second tower's collapse; I couldn't bear to ask.

There are hundreds of similar stories. Many people experienced a huge exposure to potentially damaging agents but then continued to work for days in the tedious search and rescue, or in securing the perimeter. Many had ongoing exposure to inhalation irritants, carcinogens, infectious agents and chemicals. They breathed particulates, fumes and organics that have never been studied together in terms of effects. The toxins in the 50,000 computer screens, the pulverized, aerosolized and the heated human remains, the lime in cement dust, the fiberglass and the asbestos are all a colossal problem. The smoke from the fires that flash when a beam is moved, creating a new pocket of oxygen to allow visible combustion, is also a cause for concern.

These workers returned to Ground Zero, day after day. Many went back, despite their chest tightness, cough and intermittent shortness of breath. Others denied any symptoms. Initially, their supervisors did not seem to worry about the exposures. Many officers were adamant that they must not abandon their dead and yet-to-be rescued colleagues and fellow citizens. But now they were here in the clinic, quietly asking if they had been damaged or if they would they get cancer. We had to tell them we didn't know and might not know for a long time. We encouraged those with pulmonary symptoms to be seen and treated, and not to return to "The Pile". We told them there were volunteers from around the world who would proudly take their place for a few shifts and fill the gap. With notable exceptions, this continued to be an ignored and untapped resource in many ways.

The officers talked about the opportunity to serve and protect as part of their jobs. They thought nothing of the risks they took on September 11 because they were, and are, "out there" everyday. They shrugged off our thanks to them for their having set an example for the entire country. They thanked us for caring and for being there. They really didn't see what they did at Ground Zero any differently from their other days on the job, except for the fact they were receiving embarrassing recognition for it. As one officer said, "When you pull over a car or enter an alley to investigate a complaint—something we do every day and get grief about from those involved—you are at much more risk than what we have been doing at The Pile."

7

Finding Help, Finding Answers

I became physically and emotionally exhausted after just five days. The pace was relentless. We needed more help. The political issues with the NYPD and the unions were unsolvable. The stories of heroism and grief were amazing, yet painful to hear. I was getting little sleep on the floor, especially because word got out that there was a doctor in the building. Officers who were quiet amid the chaos of the non-stop clinic activity were now open and even tearful when I spoke to them, one-on-one. I learned that sharing their concerns about mental health can often lead to a loss of routine assignments, to being forced to turn in their weapons, and to being assigned light duty. No one wanted to fail to help at Ground Zero. No one wanted a light-duty mental-health black mark on his or her record. In order to get one officer some help that he desperately needed, I encouraged him to seek counseling for his family, so that he could also receive mental health support that way, without allowing it to impact his record. (I later learned that he did follow through and was extremely grateful.)

I went home to Lancaster to recruit more assistance. I was grateful to learn that a single announcement in two churches filled a van with helpers and additional supplies. My wife, Beth, accompanied me on the return trip to NYC, and my in-laws volunteered to care for our daughters. The crew took a church van and went to manage the growing mountain of paperwork and to do data entry on six laptops loaned by Acorn Press, a company that instantly and enthusiastically gave us anything we needed. Some volunteers were trained to do the tests and others, such as Beth, to interview the officers and fill out the forms. Beth later confided in me that these interviews were some of the most compelling conversations she'd had in her life.

When it was time to get some sleep, it was a pleasant surprise to learn that word had gotten out about our efforts and that rooms had been made available for us, at no charge, at leading hotels and clubs in New York. The Lancaster volunteers slept at the Yale Club and the Mansfield Hotel. The staff thanked us "for the privilege of letting them help in this little way."

I returned home for two more breaks from the clinic over three weeks. Dr. Roberts and his key foundation people didn't take any breaks. Using a cell phone, he coordinated the expert advice and logistics of the operation. The regular phone service in Lower Manhattan was not dependable and there was no Internet access in the building. My own cell phone bill alarmed me in November, when I saw that it was over $600.

By the time the Ground Zero Clinic activities were finishing up, The Pile had been reduced from an eighty-foot tangled mess to a giant hole in the ground. With its lines of trucks, the Red Zone more resembled a construction site than the war zone we had previously seen. Everyone finally had the correct respirator masks and hard hats. Few were using the masks, however, for reasons previously mentioned.

It's important to note that the volunteers in our clinic were a fraction of the monumental volunteer effort at Ground Zero and throughout the city. The Salvation Army and Red Cross people were everywhere and helped with everything. I expected that from those two critically important groups, having witnessed their cool and efficient presence and work at significant national and community disasters over the years. The police were also served by volunteers. Two police officers—one from Toledo, Ohio, and another from Deerfield, Illinois—were there, not to win personal gain, admiration, media attention or "thank you" notes. Instead, they worked the tedious, boring, and often dangerous traffic beats and guarded water supplies to help free up the local officers for tasks they needed to do related to the attacks. I also talked with workers from the communications union, the Department of Sanitation, ironworkers, National Guard and reservists who were there to help. Some were volunteers. Others were called in as part of their jobs.

One of the most touching things I witnessed was the response of the neighborhoods. Police officers were previously not allowed to take even a cup of coffee for free. Now, in the 13th Precinct, a classic community police station that resembles the set from NBC's TV classic "Hill Street Blues," we experienced a steady stream of food brought in by families of victims, who encouraged and thanked the officers. Local restaurants and neighbors organized a continuous supply of wholesome, home-cooked food. When officers needed a break, they knew they could find something to eat without any hassle. Likewise, in the same location of the precinct hall, a supply of toiletries and underwear were available. I found myself in need of those items during the end of my first tour of duty, and a T-shirt I had grabbed during one day while working at Ground Zero had the following message scrawled on it: "Here's a hug from Toledo, Thanks." I thought of Corporal Klinger, a character from the TV show M*A*S*H who was a medic from Toledo, and I mused about what those officers in the Korean War must have endured compared to my glorified health-fair activity in New York.

My involvement as a volunteer triggered awkward, mixed feelings: appreciation, a desire to help and a sense of guilt, because I had become a part of history, but felt that I had done little to deserve this role. Sometimes I felt almost like a small-time celebrity who had the privilege to be in the midst of real heroes. It was as though astronaut Neil Armstrong had said, "Son, why don't you come along with me to the moon?" Or as if Derek Jeter had invited me into the Yankees' locker room to celebrate a World Series victory.

To put it simply, I soon realized that I was in over my head. In fact, that had become apparent the first day I went down to Ground Zero. I had borrowed an NYPD identity card and made my way past nine checkpoints to find myself wandering around at the base of the ruins. Because there was no way for civilians to get clearance to enter Ground Zero's Red Zone that first day, I had borrowed the ID from a grateful officer who wanted me to see for myself what officers were being exposed to at the site. Looking back on that incident later, I could have been arrested for impersonating an officer, gaining unlawful entry to a crime scene and possible conspiracy to commit terrorism. This was far out of my realm of experience.

While trained as a pulmonary expert, I had little experience in occupational exposures such as those afflicting the officers. I needed help beyond the chaos that was overwhelming the authorities, who released conflicting reports—reports of which the officers were highly skeptical and distrustful.

What to do when you find yourself in uncharted territory? We all—each of us in America—felt this way on September 11. What do we do in response?

8

Danger: Roadblocks Ahead

I sought—and continue to seek—opinions from experts who have set up command posts at the site. The EPA, FEMA, the New York State Health Department, the City Health Department, NYPD, FDNY, the U.S. Secret Service and others are all there. I continue to get conflicting reports on the presence or levels of asbestos, beryllium, dioxin, particulates and carbon monoxide. People have expressed concern about the contents of the pulverized and burned computer screens (50,000 of them), insulation and human remains.

To get help, I turned to the network of experts that my company had been lining up to help with writing some of its curriculum. I began to ask for assistance in finding ways to use it to address first responders' inhalation and occupational injury issues.

Dr. Edward Rosenow assisted and referred me Mayo Clinic experts in the field of occupational disease. Dr. Paul Enright, who is now working with the CDC and with NIOSH, got my staff hooked into a working group that is trying to assess and advise local doctors on how to treat people in the Lower Manhattan neighborhood. Their assistance, and the help of those to whom they referred us, allowed us to create a tele-education and telemedicine resource for reliable information to instruct the officers, conduct the screening studies and get the clinical measurements interpreted without overtaxing the local healthcare teams.

The School Education Project we were developing at InnerLink had instantly converted to become part of a disaster response program without a hitch. The White Paper demonstrated how valuable that preparation is to help with any disaster response. What we had lacked was instant access—or, for that matter, any access—to the officers' medical records.

It became clear that the online record we were using for the school project to teach children and school nurses about the terminology would be useful in a situation like this. Our call to Dr. Peter Yellowlees in Australia led him to call the president of a company in New Zealand, DoctorGlobal. They immediately called me to see how they could help, offering free lifetime use of their medical records, for the officers to use for their care, and for us to use to reduce the logistical difficulty of building a database for a study of the health effects in the future.

The biggest challenge, however, concerned legal issues. The NYPD and the six unions that represented the police officers tiptoed around the issue of on-the-job injuries and what those would mean to the officers' pension, workman's compensation and retirement plans. Other roadblocks existed, as well. Lacking any registry of local physicians trained and willing to help, we took the initiative and contacted some doctors at the major medical centers. These doctors were either too busy or too uninterested to assist in the volunteer effort. Some were concerned about their malpractice coverage and some appeared more interested in publicity or grant funds than in the patients. Out-of-state assistance in interpreting the medical tests was met with resistance from lawyers representing the some of the professional societies. Fortunately, many of these societies are gearing up for future disasters and are addressing the issues that impaired a greater response in this one. Other groups, like the American Association of Respiratory Therapists, rallied to send their members to New York, despite issues concerning licensing.

The Lancaster volunteers observed the funeral of one of the police officers. It was held at the largest cathedral in the city, yet there was still an overflow crowd. The streets were lined with uniformed officers. The bagpipes droned on in sadness. For those who did not actually get to Ground Zero but were working with the officers, it added meaning to the work we were doing and a bit of closure—if there is such a thing—on the experience.

Later that day, the group went to the Rockefeller Center and the NBC studios. We then learned that anthrax had been discovered at NBC studios, and that our group may have been exposed. Another act of terrorism had hit New York, and now the immediacy—and the ongoing nature—of the danger was all too real.

9

The Next Steps in New York

After the exposure scare at NBC studios, bioterrorism was on our minds. Fortunately for the volunteers, they had not been exposed to anthrax. But this did not mean that the issue of bioterrorism—or of terrorism in general—was no longer a concern. On the contrary, the officers vocalized a huge concern about how they could become better prepared to face future possible attacks—bioterroristic and otherwise.

The events at NBC had not spurred my first conversations about bioterrorism in New York. Three weeks earlier, as I slept with the rescuers in the Police Academy building, several officers who were responsible for training had lamented their lack of experience in dealing with anthrax if it became a problem. Many of the Hazardous Material (HazMat)-trained staff had been killed in the collapse of the Twin Towers. The officers worried that they would not have the materials or methodology to rapidly train the entire department if necessary.

There was no system in place, and no experts to call on. As Dr. Roberts and I planned the next steps for the screening of the officers in the future to track if any of the abnormalities were permanent, I mentioned that I had planned to share with them an overview of how computer-based training could train the department to deal with anthrax, and how telemedicine could be used to supervise a disaster scene and its initial management. One officer came in and asked, "Are you the anthrax expert?" I said that I was not, but that I was networked with people who were as close to experts as there are. (It's important to note that at this point, there was no doctor alive in America who had practical clinical experience with an actual case of inhalation anthrax.)

With that answer, he told me that I was to "be isolated and quarantined" until the training staff form the NYPD could arrive from headquarters. These are not words a doctor discussing anthrax likes to hear, especially after the exposure scare some had at NBC two days earlier.

The NYPD was desperate, asking if we could get an expert on camera for an instructional video that was to be made that evening for a.m. release to the precincts at the direction of the Chief. They did not have faith in their own medical staff to find such an expert, and allowed Archie and I to get out our cell phones and make some calls. My first call went to the CDC. They referred me to a New York expert, whom I called, and left a message. The call was never returned. Dr. Archie Roberts called a friend of his at a major New York medical center, who said that he couldn't respond to Archie's queries on such short notice. Tensions, obviously, were running high.

Dr. Ed Rosenow encouraged me to call Dr. Greg Poland, Mayo's bioterrorism expert. He immediately responded that he could be available to the NYPD via video conference. We were once again thanked for pitching in for the department. We set up a meeting to talk about helping the department with upgrading its training technology, capabilities, and expert content.

We put together a training web site and training program for the NYPD. We lined up more than $100,000 in support for the department and did a presentation for the Deputy Commissioner regarding anthrax, other bioterrorism agents and ways to upgrade the department's training methods. It takes a full year to properly in-service New York's 40,000 officers in a new technique or piece of equipment.

After an initial positive reaction, our efforts were placed on hold until after the first of the year, when a new Mayor and Police Commissioner were to take office. The potential gravity of a serious bioterrorism attack had not been fully grasped. I felt that we were lucky that a major assault on New York or any other city did not occur. At the time of this writing, the follow-up meetings are pending.

In the meantime, the NYPD officially responded to the screening by writing a "thank you" letter to Dr. Roberts that encouraged the Living Heart Foundation to cease its activities and let the officers do their own routine follow-up with their family doctors.

The unions wished to hold many screenings on an ongoing basis. The 1,756 officers we screened were only a tiny fraction of the officers we found with significant Ground Zero exposures. When word got out that the program was ending in two days, hundreds showed up on those last two screening days, creating a chaotic situation. The officers were upset with their management and were disillusioned. They believed that officials were covering up the type of exposure, and also the severity of that exposure. The NYPD, they sensed, seemed to fear that we were lackeys for the union who were trying to get thousands of brave men and women disability and early retirement—an act that could eventually bankrupt the city and leave it vulnerable to criminal activity.

According to some sources, some local doctors were upset with the attention our effort received. It embarrassed them to be asked why volunteers from around the country responded, when many nearby hospitals didn't assist at all with the efforts. Doctors at major New York medical centers ignored requests for help in staffing, and even ignored our requests to become New York state-licensed interpreters of the tests. When it became clear that some grant or insurance dollars might become available, these same leaders of the community lined up with grant proposals and wanted access to the confidential records of the officers we saw. At least one was heard to start a rumor that this was not a volunteer effort, and that we were getting paid for the testing, when nothing could have been further from the truth. (It should be emphasized here that the volunteers from InnerLink and from Living Heart did not receive received any compensation for their efforts at Ground Zero. In the future, should any proceeds result from the sale of this material or the use of the products or services of Project Breathe that are referenced here, they will be plowed right back into making it the best smoking prevention and national health telemedicine resource it can be.) What is planned for the NYPD at this time is not clear. Hopefully, the new Mayor and Commissioner will make informed decisions on some of the lessons learned from Ground Zero.

It is our hope that the 1,800 officers will each schedule follow-up examinations in six months and then yearly. If the group that had the worst exposure does not suffer permanent effects, then the rest of the city can "breathe" a sigh of relief. If certain conditions set in or appear later, then public health issues, including wider screening efforts, will need to be established.

What of the residents of Lower Manhattan and the exposures they endured and continue to experience? It becomes crucial that aggressive, follow-up testing of these officers and others with high exposure—such as firefighters—be conducted, for the rest of their lives, and in funded programs. What is learned from their cases will affect the care of officers who were not screened, as well as that of others in the city who have been exposed. If these exposed victims do not go on to develop chronic conditions or higher incidences of cancers, then the rest of the population with much less exposure can relax. If they do have increased problems, then expansion of screening and treatment programs needs to include citizens who worked or lived in the cloud and its fallout. It will tell the medical community about these types of exposures, given that this problem has never before occurred and very well may happen again in this uncertain world.

An anthrax and bioterrorism education program that has the capacity to rapidly in-service the entire department must be put into place. Police officers who work at collapse and fire sites do face risks, and should be treated to the same privileges as firefighters. It is my belief that every public service worker should have baseline screening as part of the job.

Records need to be accessible and an electronic medical record is one very practical and affordable means to do this. A consensus statement from the participants in the NIOSH working group will create advice to the doctors treating patients in the New York region. (A copy of the draft and updates will be posted on the Innerlinkit web site, *http://www.innerlinkit.com/lessonslearned.*)

Conflicting opinions still continue to be reported. In what I believe is the best summary publicly available at this point, ("Weighing Risks" by Max Maremont and Jared Sandberg, *Wall Street Journal*, 12/26/01), it is reported that the air is safe but many people feel symptoms. More than four hundred firefighters are now on light duty, due to health complaints. Many citizens worry about the long-term effects and secondary exposure from improper cleanup of their buildings, offices and apartments. Dioxin, lead, asbestos, fiberglass and other particulates have all, at times, been found in higher than acceptable levels. The combination of these agents with volatile organic compounds (VOCs), which are chemicals emitted when computers, carpet, and assorted other contents of buildings are burned, may be uniquely irritating.

The City of New York and the Police Department have done a phenomenal job in responding to the most devastating plane crashes and building collapses on record. They responded in heroic and dramatic ways and have shown a resiliency that is nothing short of amazing. They have had to operate in an environment of laws, regulations, unions, contracts and political limitations that still seem bizarre to me, as an outsider trying to help. They did a lot right but were also woefully ill-prepared. What happened was previously unthinkable, so one cannot pass judgment on actions that were taken in response to the attacks, but they made some mistakes. I believe they were actually living in denial about what could happen next as these things became very, very real. They were lucky, in that additional physical attacks didn't immediately occur and that bioterrorism was more of a scare than a reality. If one more significant attack or infection had immediately occurred, the city could easily have become a ghost town, as Manhattan residents became refugees to families and friends elsewhere. Some of the police I met said that in the event of a massive anthrax outbreak, they feared that drug stores would be robbed for medications and that ordinary, law-abiding citizens would consider using weapons to get antibiotics for their families, if that's what it took.

As one officer said, "If it took four days to get us adequate masks at Ground Zero, how will they get antibiotics to 200,000 people in two days? When people panic and leave the city, then some terrorists would be delighted that Americans are finally getting it and are experiencing what Palestinians have felt for a lifetime." All of these things are highly thinkable and possible today. Every community in this country needs to really think these scenarios through and be prepared for the time, as my police officer friends have chillingly said, "when the other shoe drops."

10

The National Issues

As a result of my participation at Ground Zero and my conference calls with NIOSH and CDC—as well as the research behind the White Paper I published about using schools as alternative sites for health care—I have been involved in three think tank activities related to bio-terrorism, telemedicine and homeland security. I have been part of a war games scenario involving smallpox that dealt with command and control issues, which addressed questions such as how to enforce the quarantine of a school where students have been infected. I have discussed the use of a tele-education system in schools that could become a community's telemedicine infrastructure at one-tenth the cost suggested in current plans. I have spoken with two governors and with White House staffers about these very crucial issues.

A whirlwind of interest has been generated by people in high places. It is painfully obvious that this country—and, on a smaller, but no less important scale, local communities—are ill-prepared for most emergencies.

FACT: ALL EMERGENCIES ARE, INITIALLY, LOCAL PROBLEMS.

If the local community is not prepared, people will die. On most local levels, families, companies and communities need to be equipped, trained and connected, and they must have plans to implement their responses. Baseline screening, available records, medication and supply depots, cross-trained professionals, a volunteer corps and regionalized disaster action plans are all necessary in a well-prepared community.

Governmental issues of liability and licensure need to be addressed on the macro level to allow help to flow where necessary without impeding care and expertise from across state lines. Our work in New York was offered at our own risk, given that our malpractice insurance would not cover this sort of effort outside our parent state. The doctors working at the clinic were technically in violation of New York law if they did not have a current New York license. Getting the tests interpreted and returned to the officers continues to encounter interstate legal issues, while the officers remain frightened and wonder what to do next.

The country has dedicated itself to support the New York Fire Department (America's Bravest) and the New York Police Department (America's Finest). Cards, letters and money have gushed in. Newspaper editorials have spoken volumes about those heroes. Unfortunately, other communities around the country didn't pause and take a hard look at their own local departments, which also provide 24/7 services such as safety, rescue, power, water and sanitation. It takes a brave person to go to work in mailrooms across a country plagued by envelopes laden with lethal anthrax from an unknown source. America needs to wake up and support its *local* civil servants. These are the neighbors who work weekends and holidays. They run into buildings, attach wires with electricity, search for intruders with guns and handle packages that may be deadly. Let us send cards, letters and dollars to those local groups that make America work. Let us be sure they have adequate equipment, health baselines and accessible records. Let them know you appreciate their help.

While in New York I helped hand out packages of Life Savers candies to officers and National Guardsmen guarding the train station, airport and Ground Zero. When the policemen and soldiers asked what the gifts were for, the reply was, "That's what you are, life savers! Thank you!" I challenge and invite any reader to let me feature his or her tribute to his or her local officers and civil servants in print or on our web site. Let's start a national movement and show our children that they live with real heroes every bit as brave as those in New York City.

The country needs to act and to learn how to prevent, prepare and respond to the new threats to our safety and well-being.

PART II

Lessons Learned—
A Call to Action

1

Prevent

Prevention is the best way to avoid problems in your community. There are ways to help prevent bad things from happening to you and others.

Awareness:

The first tool I learned is to BE AWARE. Look for situations that don't seem right to you; individuals who are acting suspicious and events that seem out of the ordinary should be reported. People taking flying lessons who don't care about landing a plane could be hijackers in training. Excessive purchases of fertilizer by non-farmers could suggest a bomb factory. Laboratory supplies requested by individuals without proper credentials may be a sign that a biological factory for terrorist organisms or chemicals may be under construction.

Avoidance:

When something is suspicious, avoid it at all costs and ask the authorities to investigate. A suspicious package should never be picked up, opened, tasted or shaken. Do not disturb what could be a bomb. Do not confront what may be a deranged individual. Always avoid them, and report your suspicions to the authorities.

Be well:

Wellness is more than just a trendy concept; it is a matter of survival. Forty percent of deaths by firefighters at a fire are not caused by burns or smoke inhalation; they are caused by heart attacks on the scene. We all need to be as physically fit as possible—and we need to know how to maintain that fitness, so that if an unexpected event occurs, we will be able in the best shape possible, and have the best chances to emerge from the situation unharmed.

The more we understand about the form and function of the body, the more likely we are to avoid making poor choices that will compromise our health. To prevent a disastrous outcome when exposed to an emergency, we need to incorporate an aggressive wellness program into people's lives that informs them, gets them fit, and ultimately, increases their survival. We do not know if we will need to run a great distance, carry an injured person, overcome a bioterrorism-induced infection or breathe toxic fumes. Wellness, then, requires being fit and smart.

What follows is a list of specific suggestions to help prepare you and your loved ones for the unexpected:

TIP LIST: PREVENT

Awareness and avoidance are the simplest things that facilitate prevention. Sometimes you can't avoid being in the midst of a disastrous situation. Plan on how to deal with those situations. At first glance, these recommendations may seem extremely simplistic, and there's a reason for that—they are! You may already be aware of many of them. However, unless you prepare yourself with a firm plan in mind regarding how you will before disaster strikes, you may not be able to act in the way that you hope to when stress levels, adrenaline, and confusion run high. A definite plan, therefore, is key.

Below are some simple, common sense tips to start to get you thinking about how you can best plan to become—and remain—healthy and safe.

- Get smart about your body. Learn everything you can learn about what you need to do to get fit and stay in shape.

- Then do it. Get fit and stay in shape.

- Eliminate inequalities in your community. The greater the sense of kinship that your community has generated in peacetime, the less of a challenge it will face in a difficult situation, when people are hungry or desperate.

- Be aware of health and safety risks that you may face.

- Be aware of escape routes in your place of work, your place of worship, and any building/facility where you regularly spend time. If you are vacationing in a hotel, glance over the fire exit diagram. It only takes a moment, and it is smart and conscientious to do so.

- Be conscious of health hazards—such as chemical leaks or toxic fumes at a work site, and so on—and if they are true risks to your health, avoid them, wherever possible.

- If you sense you are at risk in any situation, remove yourself from the questionable environment at the soonest opportunity, whenever possible.

- If you suspect a person or package is suspicious in some way, leave it/him/her alone. Then leave the area and notify authorities.

- If the air is contaminated (thick, dusty, hard to breathe, or you can smell foul odors):

  - Hold your breath and leave the area.

  - If the area is too large to leave, limit your time there.

  - If you must stay there, obtain and use provided masks from the authorities. If none are available, make the best mask you can, using a wet piece of cloth, pulled tightly over your face.

For a full and up-to-date list of recommendations, see our links to the FEMA web site, at **www.innerlinkit.com/lessonslearned.**

2

Prepare

All emergencies are local events, at least initially, so look at your preparation from the perspective of yourself as an individual, and that of your family, school, company and community. Each requires a detailed preparation and plan. Relevant to all these categories are health, survival, communication and evacuation issues. Adequate preparation, and incorporating those preparations into a daily routine that you can maintain, is an important element of being prepared.

When the former Soviet Union collapsed in a (relatively) peaceful economic and governmental implosion, its people found themselves without the most basic needs. Recent interviews with Brian Long, who worked with the USAID in Armenia at the time the World Trade Towers collapsed on September 11, unearthed frightening stories of survival. The interviews also revealed a worldwide compassion for the loss America experienced.

When the Soviet Union dissolved, people awoke to the reality that their currency was suddenly useless. Trucks did not deliver food. Electricity and water supply ceased for as long as two years in some regions. People resorted to burning their furniture for heat. The societal impact of an economic collapse required the Russian people to draw on a resilient resourcefulness, if they were to survive. Engineers and professors soon found themselves without professional standing and employment, but did whatever menial job was necessary to support their families. The ages of family members became irrelevant, since anyone capable of working could bring home food or firewood. Students in schools who could translate became some of their community's most valuable and highest-paid resources.

Many of our parents or grandparents in this country survived the Great Depression. Their resourcefulness, and the willingness of their families and communities to pull together, helped them make it through the tough times. I challenge you to interview and learn from someone who has been through hardship, and learn how they dealt with it. (We will discuss the importance of this concept in greater detail in Chapter 3.)

I don't mean to give an impression that we are in a doomsday situation. To the contrary, our nation is much better prepared to deal with emergencies or disasters than most. Part of the success at Ground Zero was the evacuation preparedness of the building and its occupants because of plans and procedures put in place, rehearsed and followed after the bombing there in 1993.

Even so, although the 2002 disaster in New York was incomprehensible, it was confined to a relatively small area, yet it still took four days to get appropriate masks to the NYPD rescuers. And it required an outside group of volunteers to fill the medical gap in identifying and screening those officers for respiratory illness. As this is being written, we are at war, but most of us have no true concept of hardship unless we live or work in the Pentagon, Lower Manhattan, or have a family member in public service or in the military. Preparation needs to take place at the local level, because until the government can come in and respond, local resources will have to deal with the problem. Prepare to be on your own for a while if another wave of terrorism or attack occurs.

A recognized mechanism for preparation is to practice technology and procedures frequently, so that rescue efforts for an emergency runs as smoothly as a serious drill. A fire drill or an evacuation drill is an example. I propose that we put into place the mechanisms to use technology—such as our computers, Internet service and even cable TV channels—to become part of the education and medical infrastructure.

A computer outfitted with educational and clinical diagnostic instruments can be part of that infrastructure. My company's machine is one solution—using a computer outfitted with educational and clinical diagnostic instruments that, when disaster strikes, becomes a site where care can be rendered under expert advice until advisors arrive—but there are also many other uses of conventional and advanced technology and expertise, and these need to be implemented.

To see a brief tip list of how to prepare your family or community, see Appendix I of this book, or visit the links section of **www.innerlinkit.com/lessonslearned**, *and click on the "supporting documents" hyperlink to view the Federal Emergency Management Agency web site lists.*

3

Respond

Response does not need to be heroic or immediate. It simply needs to be helpful and not caught up in ego, politics or legal considerations. Take care of the needs of your own family members first, so they do not significantly burden the system. Team up with other families or neighbors to create a larger "family". Be resourceful and prepared to change the way you do things, so that you can better help your community. If electricity or water resources are limited, flush less often, bathe less frequently and do so with fewer lights on.

If you have prepared yourself with knowledge, supplies and the right attitude, there is no need for panic and uncertainty. Control the things you can control. Have a plan to deal with those you can't. Be a leader in your circle of influence and approach the future with a calm, organized and resourceful attitude. Be prepared to encounter and aid others who are not as prepared as you are. Don't be afraid to be patriotic, and listen to the advice of our leaders.

Keep an open mind regarding the chances for a better world and support efforts like the World Anthem. (See ***www.innerlinkit.com/ lessonslearned***). The world is a smaller place, thanks to telecommunications, the Internet—and intercontinental ballistic missiles. Around the world, people lost loved ones in the World Trade Center, and in other terrorist attacks. Be tolerant of others and avoid racial profiling. Learn as much as you can about those we live with. Show that tolerance openly, and use your influence with peers to see that they promote world peace, not inhibit it.

There is a human desire to help that also heals. It feels good to give the right holiday gift. It feels even better to give of one's self during a community disaster. By responding when asked in New York, I gained a sense of satisfaction that was as great as anything I had done in my professional career. What surpassed that was the knowledge that I helped others to do the same by creating a simple way for them to step in and assist our efforts in Lower Manhattan, by enabling them to help interpret medical tests in Arizona and to copy and organize thousands of pages of medical records in Lancaster, thereby allowing experts to evaluate and study them. I received calls and notes from dozens of people thanking me for affording them the privilege of helping in the disaster.

TIP LIST: RESPOND:

- Be prepared to personally assist as a volunteer with your skills. Take classes to improve your skills.

- Join fire companies or ambulance services, or support these services in any way that you can.

- Call your community policing officer at the Police Department and see if there is a Block Watch program or Community Emergency Response Team in your neighborhood.

- Don't assume that authorities are prepared to handle a particular emergency, or that are aware of your availability for that emergency. Volunteer your services.

- Make it easy for others to volunteer by organizing a response to emergencies. These emergencies can be an immediate or long-standing need. It is often more heroic, in my mind, to do the routine, thankless tasks that don't make the headlines or lead to medals and honors.

- Give generously—whether that means blood, dollars, letters of support or time.

- Don't be afraid to do routine tasks in order to free up more highly skilled people to do the dangerous or glamorous tasks.

- Take on extra work to allow family members or co-workers to volunteer for the benefit of the community.

- Be prepared to capture data on the injured and the rescuers for current care and future study purposes.

- Start today by writing to your local proactive service or utility agency with a letter of appreciation, and encourage others to do the same.

- Be tolerant of others.

- Pray and support your religious leaders and institutions.

- Don't be afraid to show your patriotism.

- Consider asking for a curriculum program for your schools like Project Breathe, and be prepared to be added to the necessary lists of mentors, volunteers, and help support its outreach activities in community health and community preparedness.

- Consider asking your schools if they have implemented an updated on-line disaster planning and response manual that can be shared with first responders and authorities in emergency situations.

PART III

The Freedom Generation

1

What's next? How do we react to all that has happened? How do we deal with the ubiquitous warnings and fear? Is there anything to learn from the past?

I think there is. I think there is an opportunity to make a change that will mark our time as a turning point in history.

To understand this, we first need to understand where we are, in terms of the past and future. Let me offer this brief and simple review of the terminology we've used in generations past to address monumental changes over the last sixty years.

After World War II, there was a sense of euphoria in this nation. In the wave of enthusiasm that defined the Fifties, parents had children, and looked toward their future with great hope. The war was over and freedom was assured.

It was a tremendous turning point. We had come close to losing it all. In Europe, a generation of Jews and others were systematically destroyed and nations were invaded and overrun. A madman and his confused, but determined, followers became part of the worst genocide in human history.

In the Pacific, a determined Japanese army had held a similar, imperialistic view of the world. In order to defeat them, over 50,000 Americans had eventually lost their lives. Perhaps a million Japanese died in the war, including victims of deployment of two nuclear bombs that Americans developed and used in its effort to win the war. Fighting as a team, despite the prejudice and oppression in America, races had worked together to achieve victory.

That, too, was an amazing and inspiring time in our collective history.

As I've mentioned earlier, my father fought in the Battle of Iwo Jima. He was an Italian-American who served as a medic for an all African-American division. In the Battle for Iwo Jima—a small island in the Pacific that was strategically significant, since its location offered an opportunity to mount an air assault on Japan—the troops needed to make repeated landings on a hostile beach to take the island. The soldiers got to shore in landing crafts piloted by the Army's 41st Truck Battalion, the Negro Army division that drove the amphibious landing vehicles. (It's important to remember that in those days, the races were segregated and the term "Negro" was in our commonplace, utilitarian vocabulary.) With multiple boats lost and in constant fire, they continued for over four days, operating in harm's way. Their heroism generated the successful landing that fueled a turning point in the war. Finally, that battle was won, but not until over 10,000 Americans and at least that many Japanese lost their lives.

The GI's came home. They bought houses and were determined to live normal lives. They took jobs or went to school. They had children in such abundance that their offspring became part of what is known as the "Baby Boom Generation". They wanted to create a world of abundant opportunity for their children. It took some time for them to start learning how to live together across ethnic and racial boundaries, but the Boomers worked to teach their parents a new way of thinking. The Civil Rights Movement made inroads, and began to fill the gaps between the races, and to eliminate the need for hyphenated descriptions that categorize the kind of Americans each of us are.

Unfortunately, this did not mean the end of war; American soldiers were next sent to Korea, and then to Vietnam. The Boomers became college graduates and skilled tradesmen. The women of this generation rebelled against traditional role-casting and stereotypes and showed the world that they had a contribution to make. Both men and women worked hard to show their patriotism by expressing their political and social views. The more liberal and extreme of these became known as "hippies," and "radicals," to name just a few. Some protests were peaceful, and some protests resorted to violence and civil disobedience. It was a turbulent time.

During this era, technology advanced, and began to bring the peoples of the world closer. Communications technology created universal experiences and events that defined our generations, shaping our time and perspectives of the world. Television, in particular, revolutionized the way that we collectively experienced national and world events, allowing us all to potentially experience both important and trivial happenings at precisely the same time, in a much more personal way. In contrast to radio and newsprint, television had the ability to bring images and sound of real, live people and places directly into our homes—right into our personal space. (This is why some fans of popular TV sitcoms and soap operas often feel as though they "know" the actors and actresses on the show, and also why receiving distressing news from a trusted, favorite TV news anchor is often a more comforting experience than reading the same news story, written by a favorite newspaper columnist.) Events that we each watch on television at the same time, from the comfort of our own homes, become common memories that we all share (as in, "Did you see that TV show last night...?"). Those memories are, in turn, experiences that we all share together, as a nation.

All Americans of a certain generation therefore remember where they were when President Kennedy was shot. They remember next witnessing a murder, live, on TV when Lee Harvey Oswald, the man accused of shooting the president, was himself shot. Those Americans were collectively amazed by the space program and can recall the awe of watching a man walk on the moon. They were bewildered by the images of the Vietnam War, which was—by the wonders of the new technologies of television—brought into their living rooms.

We Americans were worried that the evening news "body counts" from the Vietnam War—which suddenly seemed more personal, when we learned of them through living-room-broadcast/televised programs—might someday include us. Some of us ran away to avoid the draft. Many "freaked out" and were lost to a drug and sex underground counter-culture that believed that we were all going to die anyway, so why care?

As technology advanced, new high-tech innovations became part the way of life in America. TVs, VCRs, inexpensive telephones and air travel that anyone could afford, personal computers, and eventually the Internet created new ways to learn or earn.

While some boomers focused on the war, others focused on their own successes and those of their children. Those who became obsessed with their own self-improvement efforts in the 1970s became part of what was labeled the "Me" generation. Those who became obsessed with their careers in the 1980s became known as YUPPIES (Young Upwardly Mobile Professionals). When this generation went on to have children, some referred to them as the "yuppie puppies". These children, often labeled as spoiled individuals, were criticized for failing to focus on social issues or issues of national interest, and choosing, instead, to concentrate on optimizing their own well-being.

As it grew older, this generation became known as Generation X. Growing up without a focal point, the X'ers—sometimes also called the "Me Generation"—have not yet left a significant mark on the American scene.

What of the current generation of Americans? We have a chance to make a difference, but we need to work quickly. Changes—both dramatic and subtle—are rapidly in motion. Today's students have seen defining events in their schools, and in their lives. They saw the Columbine High School shooting in 1999 and watched in horror as fellow students reportedly murdered for thrill, and out of revenge, due to peer pressure, social isolation and ridicule. Students saw their classmates murdered by peers who, many say, were numb to the gore and horror because they were repeatedly exposed to hate and death via misused technology such as movies, TV, computer games and Internet communications. After more events occurred, and the "Safe Schools" federal funding programs got started, students saw their schools become "secure facilities".

We all watched the images of the Twin Towers getting hit by aircraft. We held our breath—realizing that we were watching thousands of people die—as we saw the buildings collapse. We cried as we wondered how we would guide our children through the initial news of the events, and then prepare them for a lifetime in which they may always need to doubt about their own safety.

Look at how it has changed us. We define our world in terms of pre- or post-9/11. Our travel plans have changed. Some of us haven't traveled since that infamous day. Some of us do, but believe that the security inspection isn't as aggressive as it should be, and we are amazed that citizens can get on a train without first undergoing rigorous inspections.

Before September 11, those inspections would have caused us concern about the intrusion on our privacy rights. Now most of us have agreed to give many of these privacies up, in the interest of safety. Where once we were carefree while vacationing, we now worry as we drive through a tunnel. We thought we had gotten past the prejudices of previous generations, but many of us find ourselves looking a little differently at the fellow citizen or tourist with a Middle Eastern profile or accent.

We live in a new era. Our leaders tell us we are mounting a war on terrorism. We attack an entire country in an effort to destroy one man and his followers. We don't even dare to question how the rest of the world sees this. It may not even occur to us, as we find ourselves swept up in such an intense wave of patriotism, the likes of which I've never before seen.

New forms of weapons have appeared on the horizon. Airplanes, for example, are now used as weapons of mass destruction. We now know that pharmaceutical labs and kitchen appliances are capable of making war-grade chemical and biological weapons that can kill thousands. Soon after the September 11 attacks, we got a taste of the scary realities of biological warfare when we experienced the anthrax mail episodes. The words "dirty bombs"—bombs that contain nuclear materials, as well as conventional explosives, allowing them to spread radiation quickly when they explode, and possibly make the explosion sites unlivable—have made their way into our national vocabulary.

The enemy—that group of persons that works to harm us—hates Americans often without ever meeting Americans in person, based on partial truths, misunderstandings and years of historical issues. This enemy believes that the ultimate glory and assured way to everlasting life is to commit suicide while becoming a homicidal weapon himself, or herself. Our government warns us that we must question when, not if, the next terrorist attack will occur.

These are depressing and difficult things to think about. We have reached a transition point—a time that will influence the nation and the world. How, then, will we respond?

We can retreat into a cynical "like, whatever," or "Who cares?" attitude. We can act like spoiled victims, declaring that it's not fair that we have inherited a screwed-up world with problems that seem beyond our influence. It would be easy to just give up and say, "Why bother to study or prepare for a career?" or "Why work out or stay in shape?" and drown ourselves in commercialistic diversions—and anything else—that make us forget our worries for a while. Sex, drugs, cigarettes, and alcohol can seem tempting when looking to alleviate the pressure of overwhelming problems, especially when one realizes that more injuries, threats, attacks, or events are very likely to continue to happen in this ever-shrinking world. It is therefore no wonder that some turn to substance abuse when the pressure is high. But is this the answer?

The decisions we make will define us. We need to act; to create our own histories, and we need to do it now.

As I give lectures to school groups, I often reference my memories of significant events that were remembered by all of my classmates. Between April 1999 and September 11, 2002, when I quizzed students about their common memories, they uniformly mentioned the 1999 mass shooting at Columbine High School. In the post-9/11 era, the terrorist attacks have replaced Columbine as the unifying socio-educational experience. Based on this feedback, it would seem that today's students have no positive experiences in common. There is no John Glenn orbiting Earth for them to remember; no walk on the moon, no fall of the Berlin Wall. They have no positive histories from which to draw a positive collective sense of themselves.

It's our time to define our collective history. We can drop out and become disparaging; we can be the adults and children and teens who were alive at the turn of the millennium—a millennium that leads to the loss of freedom and the rule of fear. We can be the ones who watched as a few changed the lives of many; as ignorance led to hate; as technology enabled communication of mass hysteria and destruction, and its ability to promote understanding and peace went largely ignored. We can be known as Generation L, the post-911 Lost Generation.

Or we can stand up and do better.

My vision is that we use the September 11th attack as the ultimate learning opportunity. Let us become known as Generation F, The Freedom Generation.

We must strive to collectively remember and archive life in the Pre-911 era. We must learn how to prevent, prepare and respond to threats on our safety and way of life. We must learn how to become part of the solution. This means taking the initiative to embrace our counterparts in other cultures, allowing them to get to know and understand us, and we them.

We need to have a worldwide solution to a worldwide problem. The Freedom Generation, then, needs to be not just an American phenomenon, but an international one, as well. It needs to be an international movement of open-minded people who strive, together, to insure abolition of ignorance and advancement of true freedom and peaceful coexistence.

Is this a realistic goal? Some of our country's greatest leaders have thought so. President Kennedy believed in these ideals, and he backed up these beliefs when he initiated the Peace Corps. President Eisenhower held those same beliefs, as he demonstrated when he established the People to People Student Ambassador Program. President Carter expressed his support for this ideology through his post-term work with Habitat for Humanity. Likewise, the current administration is brilliant in its leadership in creating the Freedom Corps as the parent organization for dozens of organizations and programs that promote shared experiences and volunteerism.

What can we do to help? I propose that we start with ourselves. Let's remember what life was like before the events of September 11. Before the post-911 changes altered our level of privacy and freedom—before our sense of fearful travel—we had a different mindset. It is important that we do not forget this. It is important that our freedoms aren't eroded, bit by bit, as we become accustomed to the next newest approach to protecting us from ourselves, and from our enemies. We need to preserve an America that we are proud to call America.

Preserving this freedom means understanding it, and keeping track of what it means. My father's generation is losing its World War II veterans—and the citizens that supported them from the home front—at a faster rate than it lost them from the carnage during the war. These soldiers and their loved ones endured depression prior to the war and then the threat of nuclear attack in the decades that followed. Their wisdom and mistakes are what created the successes and advances that we have today and the problems that have not yet been solved. We need to become aware of their collective wisdom, fears, prejudice, advice and contributions.

I challenge you to make the time to interview your parents, grandparents and neighbors, and so on (or start a journal of your own, if you are rich with experiences, and prefer this route). Read about the challenges they've faced in their lifetimes, and become knowledgeable about what was going on in the news during the decades in which they've lived. Ask them how they contributed to maintaining freedom for us to enjoy. If they were a veteran, or knew one, ask them to relate these experiences. What type of commitment or sacrifice did they endure? What did people at home suffer to support them?

Archive these stories with your own notes, articles, stories, poems, or pictures; use technology to record the voices or images of those you interview. The insight you gain into yourself, your generation, your place in history, and your loved ones will be priceless. The recordkeeping will be valuable to you (and possibly them) someday.

Telling our stories, understanding and preserving our past, understanding and appreciating our own freedom and creating our own history are extremely important, then, when we decide what kind of life we are going to have for ourselves, as a generation, and as individuals.

Another important task that faces the Freedom Generation lies in ensuring not only the survival of its historical roots, but in ensuring the survival of the self. You need to make sure that you, (and, with you, your stories, and your understanding of history and freedom) actually survive; otherwise, you will not be able to contribute to the future, nor enjoy the benefits of that future. Each of us must therefore learn how to take care of ourselves, our families and our communities in this new era in which we live.

This sense of responsibility also extends to the community, and the institutions and organizations within the community. The institutions where we all go to school, work, or live must put plans in place and take seriously the concept of prevention and preparation for emergencies. Taking care of ourselves, then, means getting plans in place to handle unexpected events within our local governments and local communities—our neighborhoods, our scouting organizations, schools, churches, block watches, CERT organizations and so on—as well as our families and ourselves.

On a more individual level, we can all optimize our chances of survival if we get ourselves in good physical and emotional shape prior to a challenging event. Therefore, learning as much as one can about how the body works and how to prevent injury is a responsibility each of us in this generation needs to take. We can not expect others to risk their lives and resources in rescues and therapies if we can not exercise the discipline to learn and then make the right decisions to optimize our own health, day by day.

Reducing the risk of becoming injured—and increasing the likelihood of being able to escape a dangerous situation unharmed, and possibly even help others in need, if necessary—is extremely important, and could ultimately save not only your life, but the lives of many others you may help along the way, as well.

I learned through my experiences at Ground Zero that when there is a need for someone to help, it is a great feeling to be able to step up and do so. If there is an opportunity to use your particular skills, then find a way to use them. Study first aid and become an Emergency Medical Technician. If technology is your skill set, why not learn how to be sure your community has the up-to-date information it needs for any emergency? Why not consider setting up telemedicine support for the health care workers? If you are able-bodied, why not become cross-trained in the use of a fire hose or learn how to perform traffic control, so professionals with other skills can be freed up to solve other problems?

Proper training is key. Be sure that what is needed for the emergency, or the extraordinary event, is so familiar to you that you will not require additional instruction on the spot. Use your creativity to find ways to reinforce your new abilities as you perform everyday routines, so that your skills will be sharp and your responses will be automatic, sure and calm, should you be called to action. Volunteer to be trained, and trained well. Ask your organization to provide instructional support, in terms of both manpower and finances. Rely on yourself and volunteer your services to the community. Encourage others to do so, and soon you will live in a community that will have a common vision, that will work well together, even in extraordinary times.

I think it is reasonable to assume that the American way of life will survive, even in times of great struggle and challenge. But what of the subtler, less dramatic goals to which the Freedom Generation can aspire?

We need to find ways to use our skills in all disciplines, to bridge the gaps in our own society and to extend those bridges around the world. Would Dylan Klebold and Eric Harris have killed at Columbine if they had not been reportedly alienated by their classmates for years, and if they had not been possibly conditioned and trained to kill by entertainment and education technology? We must not tolerate the cruelty and peer pressure our students must face, in terms of social survival in school. Our prejudices need to be discussed and addressed; we need to seize opportunities to communicate about all pertinent issues. It will take years, and probably generations, to build the bridges I visualize, but if we miss our chance with our contemporaries, our children may not be granted the same chance.

If, however, many of us exert a consistent and focused effort to consider the implications of our actions on the community of our local and world neighborhood, we can make a difference.

This is indeed a formidable challenge, but we have the tools to help us address it. We can indeed use technology to help bridge the gaps of technology.

Because it is relatively new, we don't yet know the complete impact of the Internet's impact on our society, although it's already clear that the Internet's ability to allow individuals to cheaply and easily broadcast messages around the world is profound—and, as technology gets cheaper, this increasingly gives people of all ages, genders, races, creeds and socioeconomic strata a better chance to be heard, to be heard instantly, and to connect to people and information that matter to them with relative ease. Its ability to help set the wheels of change in motion, by linking like-minded people together as they work to solve problems, is self-evident.

For those of us who lack technical skills or knowledge base, the Internet, the virtual classroom and mentoring opportunities can often provide an opportunity that can be the first step toward a climb out of poverty. Shared databases can allow students from around the world to collaborate on issues that affect all of us. Like terrorism and its weapons, epidemics, water quality and air pollution circumnavigate the globe. Expertise from one area can be used to help solve problems elsewhere.

Be open-minded about your ability to influence others and allow yourself to be influenced by others. I believe that we must work together, or the problems of poverty, hatred, pollution or disease will reach around the neighborhood or the world, and will affect us. Your problem should also be my problem. Opportunities to learn from, and even communicate with colleagues around the world—in their own language!—exist, and can enable each one of us to learn to be a part of the solution.

We live in a time when we have a greater-than-ever ability to share an opinion, influence another or gather information. The average citizen of the world with a computational device and connection to the Internet can influence, or be influenced by, millions. We need to continue to be creative in positive ways to use this powerful new resource and tool.

All of us in The Freedom Generation need to weave into our own consciousness the desire to volunteer. This means helping to solve not only our own problems, but also each other's. There are abundant opportunities and programs of which we may take advantage. If we are to be a part of a solution, then thinking creatively becomes part of our core. We use our muscles to build, our technology to lessen digital divides in opportunity, our companies to create quality jobs as we create new drugs, pollution control and lesson waste in the way we design products, and our neighborhoods to help raise all of the community's kids as we help look out for the neighbors' kids, just like our parents did. We can all contribute at work, at play, in faith, and in the community.

Finally, when things need to be fixed, communities need to pull together. New York did it, as the entire USA—and, in fact, the world—became part of the New York solution in an act of volunteerism and donation. We now realize that unchecked pollution, AIDS, nuclear war, and terrorist release of smallpox on an uninocculated world can end humanity. The immense pain, anger, fear and trepidation, horror and amazement of that Ground Zero experience have taught us valuable lessons. Let us take what we have learned and become known as the people who helped turn the tide on centuries of war, leading the next generations into centuries of peaceful collaboration in an ever-shrinking world.

In years to come, let it be said that the Freedom Generation taught us how to solve problems together, and in doing so, started the process of healing for future generations. Let future historians judge that The Freedom Generation acted to fight for worldwide human rights and create a world where people could live in peace, and experience the Freedom we inherited from our forefathers and mothers. Let it be said that one of the Lessons Learned at Ground Zero was that the most effective weapon may not be an act of war, but an Act of Peace. Let us vow to do our part and enable the Freedom Generation to become the outgrowth of this challenging time in the history of mankind.

What are Acts of Peace? Acting out in peace does not involve seeking out an "eye for an eye," against your enemy, or even "turning the other cheek" in the face of violence. Acts of Peace involve extending a kind word or a hand and reaching out to someone. If you are a student, it means making a point of including the kid at recess who has never asked to play, or the pre-teen or teen who doesn't get invited to any parties. For anyone, at any age, it means simply working to bridge old gaps of communication, or extending a helping hand to someone in need.

On a national scale, President Franklin Delano Roosevelt created an Act of Peace when he kicked off a campaign to combat polio by asking American children to donate ten cents to the cause. President George Bush echoed this act in when he ordered that food be dropped to the people of Afghanistan and encouraged American children to send one dollar to Afghani children in need.

That effort by President Bush was not only a touching gesture, but also a much-needed campaign. According to Red Cross statistics available at the time, only twenty-three percent of the total population of Afghanistan, which was then experiencing a severe drought, had access to safe water; twelve percent lived in adequately sanitary conditions and only nineteen percent of rural dwellers had access to clean water. In a November, 2001 Sunday radio address, President Bush voiced the philosophy of an Act of Peace perfectly, saying, "This is something the children of America can do for the children of Afghanistan, even as we oppose the brutal Taliban regime. We will oppose their evil with firm justice, and we will answer their hatred with compassion for the Afghan people." He later emphasized this sentiment, saying, "Children across America can help their peers in a country of innocent children who have gone without for so many years."

How can we commit an Act of Peace, on a personal level? An Act of Peace does not have to be a grand gesture. It can be something as simple as becoming part of a church or Freedom Corps activity. And starting to volunteer.

As a first step, vow to take care of yourself, learn to take care of others, take charge and become prepared and get involved to help where you can. Create your own acts of kindness, generosity and compassion. Added together, these small acts will create a groundswell and a signature of a generation that solves problems together in small ways to preserve the sense of freedom that we all must strive to remember and keep alive. This sense of freedom and goodwill becomes the basis for Acts of Peace. This is the real *Lesson Learned at Ground Zero*. The world outpoured its caring and the volunteerism, as reflected in its acts of peace. This approach can be your legacy.

When you close this book, go off and create your own small Act of Peace. Do it now; your neighbor is counting on you. So is the rest of the world.

Epilogue I

As the City of New York tries to decide what to do with its workers, police officers and citizens who have been exposed to toxic materials in the air, we will see legal, union, political and medical discussions enter into the arena. The quality of the air at Ground Zero, and the long-term health effects of all of the Ground Zero workers are not yet clear, and may not be for years to come. The recommendations for the doctors in the community who are treating those in Manhattan will continue to be updated. The scientific reports regarding these issues will continue to be released over the next several months. (We will continue to include some of these reports in our web site, as they are made available to us, at *http://www.innerlinkit.com/lessonslearned*.)

Who am I and why was I lucky enough to have had the privilege of helping in New York? Why did I bother to write this book about my experiences? I think it is because, in some strange way, many things I have done in my life have been in preparation for my trips to Lower Manhattan, and for my efforts to help America preserve homeland security. I see a void in the overall community leadership in this country, and I feel that my observations based on my experiences in New York, and even before that experience, may be of some help. I believe we need to learn from our successes and failures, as a nation. It's time to prepare—to look forward with confidence, not apprehension. Our kids and our cities need to be able to move forward safely and not to be defeated emotionally or physically by the terrorism we now subconsciously think about every time we see an airplane in the skies above, or drive our cars through a tunnel, or see someone who meets the current terrorist profile.

To understand the suggestions I make in this book, and the perspectives and observations I present, it may be useful to learn some background information about me.

I was raised by parents who were community volunteers. My parents organized an effort to raise funds for band uniforms. They orchestrated a yearly drive for Christmas gifts for kids in the ghetto and brought their children with them to deliver the goods. Their leadership, and their support of these efforts, was heroic in ways that don't make the newspaper headlines, but do make a difference.

As a Boy Scout, I achieved the rank of Eagle—primarily as a result of my parents' guidance and urging. Although I hid my involvement in Scouts from my contemporaries, I am now proud of my involvement with Boy Scouts and the patriotism and resourcefulness it taught me.

My parents made sure that the Scout troop had the necessary equipment, allowing us to learn to survive without modern conveniences, and to learn First Aid. Within a year of that training, I used those skills in a train wreck site, at which I was the only person with a First Aid background. I successfully resuscitated an injured and non-breathing man with no pulse and kept him alive until an ambulance crew could arrive an hour later. That success was only possible because of my parents' efforts with that Scout troop. Having the confidence to respond to such a situation and ultimately make a difference also influenced my decision to pursue a career in medicine.

During medical school and my residencies, I found myself motivated by teachers who loved their discipline and imparted a sense of obligation to use any knowledge acquired for the good of the community. I learned how to be resourceful with a bronchoscope in order to reach and treat difficult lung tumors. I also learned that I could solve problems by using knowledge from one discipline and then apply it to another. I found that I could combine my creativity and skills with those of people with entirely different backgrounds to create solutions to problems and that, given the right team, could form a company that could solve problems on a larger scale, out in the world. I merged a bank teller machine with a pharmacy to help cut down on drug errors in hospitals. (MedSelect Systems Division of Diebold). I applied new e-mail capabilities to telemedically treat a patient in one part of the world by allowing a doctor to assist in another (MedVision). I have used the Internet in a way that created a safe haven for kids to search without the risk of encountering pornography (EdView, now part of Apple Computer). I have been a small part of the effort to create online case-based training and make it available to the NYPD and others, and an award-winning case study on anthrax for continuing education (MedCases). Another example is the team of respiratory volunteers at our Ground Zero Clinic, which represented all walks of life, nationalities and skill levels.

In medicine, the ongoing problem-solving exercises I have faced in the past twenty years make me realize that it is not very difficult to involve a patient in the healing process in an effective way. Years of teaching patients how to avoid inhalation injury, to stay healthy on the job site, to stay fit and to know how and when to access professional help taught me how to deal with the police officers at Ground Zero. I have learned how giving a plan to a patient with end-stage lung cancer can empower him to find comfort in knowing that he will have some level of control and confidence as he faces a series of horrific adversities from his illness. A plan helps.

It is time to once again take the initiative and apply what we have learned from Ground Zero to surround ourselves with the expertise that will help prepare a frightened and ill-prepared nation.

It is my hope that we can inspire and inform people so they may survive and thrive in the challenges and uncertainty of the future.

When the first World Trade Center tower collapsed, we were all surprised. While we watched, the heroes responded. While we worried, the heroes acted. While we wondered what we could do to help, the heroes helped. Some people who responded died that day, and some are now ill or injured from the inadequate equipment and ongoing exposures during the response. If it happened in our town, would we be prepared? How would we respond? Would we support those who did? Would they be adequately prepared and protected? If so, how? What specific role can you play in that community effort? What can your association, union or company do to prepare you and your community? What can you do?

Take an inventory of what you can offer and let your local and state agencies know of your interest and skills. Be sure your Scout troop, fire company, local hospitals and schools are supported with your money, time and talent. It is heroic to give of oneself for the benefit of others. Download and use the Personal Safety Manual from the FEMA web site (**www.fema.org**). Although your role might not be as dramatic as that of a rescuer who evacuates a victim from a dangerous disaster scene, remember that it is also heroic to be one of the people who enable that rescuer to be there with the right knowledge, equipment and emotional support.

One person can make a difference. Your community is relying on you to be that person.

Epilogue II

It's happening. Nearly six months have passed since September 11, 2001. Some have forgotten, while others have acted and are continuing to show their appreciation by doing outreach education, volunteering and leading the way to a smarter, healthier and safer future.

Volunteers have reached out from our company to pitch in and help. InnerLink co-founder Martha Harris organized an appreciation morning at the Janus School in Mount Joy, Pennsylvania. This school specializes in aiding students with learning challenges. At this special event, Janus students worked to learn the roles of first responders who spent the morning with the students. The day culminated in a moving ceremony, in which the officers received a hero's tribute by the students in writing and in artwork, and on a hero's wall dedicated to them at the school. This little town's officers had tears in their eyes as they received their thanks.

A group of students testing the use of Project Breathe in the Vocational Technical school environment is presenting its appreciation to the Annville Fire Department at their Annual Dinner March 9th. This department is similar to that in more than eighty percent of the nation, in that it is composed of volunteers who have held flower sales and "Boot Drives" (collecting donations in boots at the traffic lights in their town). Other students in that class are going to use our equipment to create a baseline online, and a smart card, in-the-pocket medical record with baseline screening information the students acquire on it. While they learn about, and work with medical professionals, they are practicing their skills and providing a potentially life-saving service to the officers.

Lieutenant Tom Coleman, of the Mayor Fire Department FD Ladder Co. 131, came to the Hans Herr School in the Lampeter Strasburg School District (Lancaster, Pennsylvania), to thank the students for "Operation Socks." Students had pitched in by providing socks to the rescuers who didn't have time to go home and change. Five of the lieutenant's co-workers from his small company died inside Tower One. Surviving heroes came to the school and thanked the students. The superintendent gave the officers a pin with the letters "LS" engraved on it, to signify the initials of the school district. As he presented them he said, "It also stands for Leader/Servants. That's what you are." Lt. Coleman responded to the students, stating, "It filled our batteries and kept us going. Since September 11th, we've become the center of the world, and we've learned that the world is a very small place…as long as we are on the job, we are going to remember you."

Led by Lancaster Mayor Charlie Smithgall, City Councilman and Emergency Management Services Director Gene Duncan, and Community Police Officer William Gleason, The City of Lancaster and surrounding communities are coming together to try to create a citizen corps council. It is a network of volunteers, schools, hospitals, agencies, non-governmental organizations, first responders and community policing agencies. They will try to test the use of a networked system across the community. They will participate in creating an online mechanism for disaster planning and response, sharing information with agencies when appropriate, so that a rescuer or SWAT team will know the floor plan of a school or factory, and will therefore know where hazardous materials are stored. Schools, factories, colleges, hospitals and other agencies will be involved in this effort. This demonstration project will lead to a community where new approaches and technologies can be tried and tested. When something is found useful, we can help get the word out to other communities in the state or nation. We are working hard to develop the tools that will allow that to happen.

Momentum is running high. On February 15, 2002, I got a call from a special assistant to the President in the Office of Homeland Security with an invitation to come in for "a chat about our vision and what we are doing with our demonstration project." He mentioned that all of this might dovetail with the strong message President Bush sent to the nation in his State of the Union Address on January 29, 2002, in which he implored Americans to work to strengthen their communities through the newly proposed Citizen Corps, which is a part of USA Freedom Corps. President Bush has challenged U.S. citizens—especially teenagers—to contribute 4,000 hours of their lives (about two years) in volunteer time, energy and creativity to make Citizen Corps and this country even stronger.

Does anyone care about volunteerism and heroes and how they can make a series of small differences that lead to a movement? Can the nation weave into its fabric a new culture of volunteerism and patriotism that can create a Freedom Generation, leading us into the future with technology skills, and learning from the combined wisdom of their elders and the professionals in their community? Can we work in peacetime and in wartime to create a better America on ordinary days—in order to be ready for those potential extraordinary days? I believe we can. So do those heroes who have joined forces to make this country a safer place, or have felt the good feelings that come from volunteering.

We all have been called to action. It is our time and our turn to step up and make a difference. It is time to take charge of our own health. It's time to be as smart as we can be. It's time to share what we know. It's time to recognize, thank and support our local everyday heroes. It is time to volunteer. I believe we are all up to the challenge.

To see supporting documents and links, or to learn more, see www.innerlinkit.com/lessonslearned.

APPENDIX A

Prepare and Respond

It is crucial that you prepare yourself in ordinary times, so that you will be ready for the extraordinary. When in doubt, use this rule as your guide: *Think in terms of **being self-sufficient for 72 hours**, without supplies, or assistance.* What would you need to have on hand? What records would you need?

For the most definitive, up-to-date preparedness information, please refer to _www.innerlinkit.com/lessonslearned_, where you will find continually updated links to expert sources, including a preparedness tip list from _www.fema.gov_. As a means to get you thinking about some of the important issues concerning personal/community/family readiness, however, we have provided a supplementary list of basic guidelines that you will want to start thinking about, as you begin to become a safer, smarter and healthier person/family/community:

SOME BASIC GUIDELINES
TIP LIST: PREPARE:

A. **Prepare a collection of critical information.** Assume that your family doctor cannot be reached, your computer databases are inaccessible and your financial records are not kept by your bank or pension fund during a disaster.

    1. Print and back up critical computer information.

- Keep copies of your most recent bank or other financial statements. Assemble your medical information and have it available.

- Print critical documents

- Create backup discs on a regular basis and store them away from the computer

- If serving critical information, have a redundant server located elsewhere in another region of the country.

- Keep a personal record (in your home, wallet, or online, or consider an on-line medical record and smart card) of:
  - History of health problems
  - Immunizations
  - Allergies
  - Emergency Contacts
  - Physicians and hospitals where you routinely get care
  - Consent for emergency treatment for your children

B. **BE ORGANIZED:** Be sure you have a supply of your routine essential needs. Think through a scenario where there is no water, transportation, food, cash supply or expert help for a few days. (There are great resources that support and go beyond the content of these lists. View them from the links at the Lessons Learned portion of *www.innerlinkit.com*).

1. Medications

- Basic pain killers, antihistamines, nausea and diarrhea medicines and prescription medications

- Keep at least a one month supply of your prescription medications

2. Food
   - Nonperishable, high-energy, or nutrient-dense

3. Water
   - Bottled water, or water source other than tap
   - Purification tablets, bleach, and instructions.
   - One cap of chlorinated bleach per one gallon of water

4. Flashlights and batteries, candles and matches or lighters

5. Basic First aid supplies
   - Butterfly strips for lacerations
   - Betadyne or similar wound disinfectant
   - Band-Aids (or other gauze adhesive strips)
   - First aid handbook
   - Elastic bandage
   - Gauze and tape

6. Transportation
   - Keep the tank full of fuel
   - Keep the car similarly equipped with basic First Aid supplies, blankets and lighting

7. Communications
   - Redundant communications options will increase the chance of being informed and able to communicate
   - Cell phones
   - Internet access

- Wired land telephone
- Transistor radio
- Walkie-talkie
- Computer information (see Item #A-1)

C. BE READY FOR THE UNEXPECTED

1. Devise a plan with your family and coworkers to deal with things you can't control.

- Escape routes
- Meeting places
- Phone chains
- Web site reference to reach others
- Be calm, thoughtful, and reassuring to yourself and family

2. Be as healthy as you can be at all times.

- Absolutely no smoking: Inhalation injury is a huge risk in collapse, fire, or bioterrorism.
- Be fit: The number one cause of death in firefighters is heart attack. You may have to walk long distances, run up stairs, or carry heavy loads.

3. Family communication back up

- Phone and email. Know your family members' phone and email addresses, if applicable, and have them on hand.
- Meeting place—Designate an appropriate meeting place where your family can congregate in the event of an emergency

- Arrange for guardians or other family partners to use if current needs are not met alone

- Home fire—Delineate plans. What would you do in the event of a home fire? Where would you meet? (i.e. would you all meet in front of the next-door neighbor's house, by the mailbox?) What routes would you use to get out (you need to have several routes, depending on where the fire is). Have a family fire drill to practice.

- Contamination. Have a discussion with family members and devise a plan, based on this handbook, and other information, as recommended by the authorities, such as FEMA *(www.fema.org)*

- Separation from caretakers. Where would you meet? With whom would you meet? Designate a contact that lives out of the region as a last resort to coordinate with, or travel to, in times of extreme emergency.

Appendix B

Readers' Guides

PART ONE: BOOK CLUBS

If you're a member of a book club, you know what it's like to be the first to begin the discussion. At times, it's easy to feel tongue-tied in front of even a group of friendly bookworms! We're here to help, however. Below are some questions to help spark some lively, thoughtful and memorable Lessons Learned *conversations in your next book club meeting.*

1. If you were called to volunteer at Ground Zero, would you go? Would you do anything differently than the way the volunteers in the book did? If so, how, and why?

2. Throughout the book, Dr. Rob talks about his father, who was a medic in Iwo Jima. Why do you think that is? How are his father's experiences like those of the Ground Zero victims and first responders? Volunteers? How are they different? What does Dr. Rob's father symbolize to him?

3. Who are the heroes and angels?

4. Do you agree with Dr. Rob's assessments of the Baby Boomers, the Me Generation, Gen X and Gen Y? What do you think about his hopes for his Freedom Generation? (Part 3)

5. What do you think about Dr. Rob's statements about the health-care industry (Part 1, Chapter 3)?

6. Do you feel that the book is an effective "Call to Action"? Why or why not?

7. Discuss/react to the following quotes:

   A. *Except for the flags and the traffic, I was struck by just how normal the city seemed only a fifteen-minute walk from Ground Zero. I wondered what Gettysburg, Berlin, Pearl Harbor, Hiroshima, Seoul or Saigon looked like in the weeks and months after their infamous attacks. I developed a deeper appreciation for the challenges that previous generations had faced, and the things that they had feared. We had all endured a horrible day and it has affected us all. I hoped we would not have a series of days or years like this ahead of us.*

   B. *One officer lingers until after midnight and shares his story, asking for my advice and counsel.... He is concerned for his health, his job, his emotional condition and his family. Our visit lasted until 1:00 a.m. We conducted a visit that no doctor or patient could ever have had in today's medical machine system. We are both grateful for the visit.*

   C. *I, like many others in the country, felt impotent, frustrated and unable to help in this time of need, so I was glad to learn of a way to help. The nation gave blood and sent money, but somehow, this does not feel as fulfilling as many of us wish.*

   D. *Dirt and dust were thick in the air, and shattered glass from blown-out storefront windows and other debris were strewn all about...the cadet heard an eerie hissing sound coming from a gourmet coffee shop...he made his way toward the noise and discovered its source: the shop's cappuccino machine was running!...the cadet walked over to the machine, and started making lattes for the rest of the crew. The officers and cadets drank them quickly, their throats no longer dry. They organized a brief plan of action and moved out towards the remaining tower of the WTC to help evacuate it.*

E. *Sometimes I felt almost like a celebrity who had the privilege to be in the midst of real heroes. It was as though astronaut Neil Armstrong had said, "Son, why don't you come along with me to the moon?" Or as if Derek Jeter had invited me into the Yankees' locker room to celebrate a World Series victory.*

F. *…Unfortunately, other communities around the country didn't pause and take a hard look at their own departments, which also provide 24/7 services such as safety, rescue, power, water and sanitation. It takes a brave person to go to work in mailrooms across a country plagued by envelopes laden with lethal anthrax from an unknown source. America needs to wake up and support its local civil servants.*

G. *Those who became obsessed with their own self-improvement efforts in the 1970s became part of what was labeled the "Me" generation. Those who became obsessed with their careers in the 1980s became known as YUPPIES (Young Upwardly Mobile Professionals). When this generation went on to have children…this generation became known as Generation X. Growing up without a focal point, the X'ers…have not yet left a significant mark on the American scene.… What of the current generation of Americans? We have a chance to make a difference, but we need to work quickly. Changes—both dramatic and subtle—are rapidly in motion.*

H. *All of us in The Freedom Generation need to weave into our own consciousness the desire to volunteer. This means helping to solve not only our own problems, but also each other's. There are abundant opportunities and programs of which we may take advantage. If we are to be a part of a solution, then thinking creatively becomes part of our core.*

I.   *"Let's Roll."—Todd Beamer, hero and passenger of Flight 93, the aircraft that several courageous passengers brought down near Somerset, PA on September 11, 2000.*

PART TWO: LESSON PLANS

Lessons Learned at Ground Zero can be used as a supplementary text in many different contexts. My staff has included some sample lesson plans in this book to help spark ideas for teachers and professors who are interested in bringing this story of real-world experience into their classroom.

In addition, we are continually creating updated lesson plans based on current news events, and readers of this book may view and use updated lesson plans, in addition to the ones in this book—reflecting breaking news events around the world—so feel free to email us with your feedback about the following plans, at *info@innerlinkit.com*. You may also view future plans, since they will be added to our continually updated web site, at *www.innerlinkit.com/lessonslearned*.

Sample lesson plans included in this section:
Health (grades 7–9)
History (middle school, high school, university level)
Philosophy (AP high school/university level)
Psychology (university level)
Science (AP high school/university level)
Social studies (grades 7–9)
Sociology (university level)

Lessons Learned at Ground Zero:
Lesson Plans for the Health Instructor

Grade Level: Grades 7–9
Estimated Time: Two one-hour sessions, and one supplementary lesson

Lesson Overview:

Lessons Learned at Ground Zero is a book that chronicles a doctor's experiences while volunteering to help test First Responders who worked at the site of the World Trade Center, following the attacks of September 11, 2001. A pulmonary expert and practicing doctor for more than 20 years, the author not only recounts his personal experiences at Ground Zero as he explains the possible dangers that airborne contaminants—sent into the air by a large-impact bombing or accident of this nature—can cause, but also stresses the need for all of us to keep safe and healthy during ordinary times, so that, should an extraordinary event occur, we will be better equipped to handle it well. This advice hits home for the health teacher, who can integrate Dr. Rob's disaster preparedness/fitness advice into a wellness lesson plan, for greater impact, variety and increased informative lecture value in the classroom.

Materials:

- *Lessons Learned at Ground Zero* Checklists for Preparedness (outlined in Part Two)

Procedure:

1. In *Lessons Learned at Ground Zero*, Dr. Rob encouraged us all to volunteer in any way we can because "it feels good to help," and he encouraged the First Responders who were having a difficult time adjusting to the stress of the situation to seek help. How does increased adrenaline affect your health over time? Finding positive

activities and alleviating stress is an important part of healthful living. Encourage students to share their feelings about the events they read about—and experienced—and talk about ways they can work to effect a positive change. Ask students: What can you do to help—send socks and other supplies to rescuers, or typing up medical records, or helping to direct traffic or rescuing families from burning buildings or donating blood or pennies, or something else entirely? What other ways can you maintain emotional equilibrium when you find yourself facing stress? How does this affect your overall health? How does this affect your life, overall?

2. Why were the doctors and volunteers concerned for the health of the First Responders at Ground Zero? (Because of the toxins and particulates in the air, caused by the impact of the attacks, and the long-term effects this air pollution may have on their lungs.) Discuss the importance of lung safety, as outlined in the book. Are there any similarities between the effects after exposing the lungs, during a brief period, to the extreme pollution found at a site such as Ground Zero, and after longer-term exposure to cigarette smoke? Why is it important to maintain fitness and health, if you wish to volunteer?

3. Use the book to enrich a fitness regime lesson. Ask the students: What is the main cause of death on the job among firefighters? Why is it important for ordinary citizens to maintain fitness, in light of the events of September 11? What are some of the specific things that we can do in ordinary times to help prepare us for the extraordinary? What food choices can we make that will improve our fitness, and how can we help incorporate fitness into our daily routine, so that we can keep up an active lifestyle even in busier times? What role does hygiene play?

Assessment:

Student understanding should be assessed through:

- Contributions to class discussion

- Demonstrated understanding of the events of September 11

- Write a brief reaction essay: Why were the doctors and volunteers concerned for the health of the First Responders at Ground Zero, and what does that have to do with teen smokers? Make a case for the anti-smoking campaign.

- What are the benefits of volunteerism, in terms of stress reduction/health benefits? List three things you can do as a volunteer.

- List five ways you can improve your health and wellness; OR list five ways you can become better prepared for any unexpected event.

Lessons Learned at Ground Zero: Lesson Plans for the History Instructor

Grade Level: University Level
Estimated Time: Six one-hour sessions, or six class periods

Lesson Overview:

The attack on America on September 11, 2001 constituted a seminal moment in modern American history. This lesson plan poses important questions that all historians and history students must ask in this post-9/11 era, as we all work to place the Attack on America, and subsequent events, in context with the past.

Materials:

- *Lessons Learned at Ground Zero*

- Access to further research materials (Internet, library) for at-home writing assignments

Procedure:

1. The attack on America on September 11, 2001 was a defining moment in modern American history. Ask students to share what they know about the event. What historical significance, if any, did the terrorists attach to the September 11 date, and why? What are the religious, socioeconomic, cultural and historic roots of this terrorism? Why did the terrorists choose the World Trade Center—and, for that matter, America—as their target? Why did they use commercial airlines? What does the author, Dr. Rob (Gillio), suggest that American citizens do, on an interpersonal level, to combat the terrorist movement? Do the students agree with his solutions? Are they historically sound? Why or why not?

2. In *Lessons Learned at Ground Zero*, Dr. Rob discussed his father's experiences at Iwo Jima in relation to his experiences at Ground Zero. Ask students to relate other instances of terrorism and shared traumatic experience in modern history. How are the events of 9/11 similar to other conflicts we have seen throughout history? How are they different? Do we face any challenges today that previous generations did not need to consider? How do issues such as new weaponry, access to information, bioterrorism and technological communications affect your answer?

    How has technology impacted international relations? How has it impacted peacemaking efforts, and wartime strategies? How has it impacted intelligence-gathering?

3. As far as they are able to tell at this time, can the students think of any other events in history with similar impact to the nation as the events of September 11, 2001? Does contemporary reaction to major events such as these vary throughout history, and from culture to culture? Give examples. Does political/cultural/religious climate play a part, and if so, how?

4. What is the history of volunteerism in America? How have volunteers shaped our country, from earliest times to today? Ask students to think of examples when volunteers have stepped in and filled important roles in American history, created/driven important movements, etc. What is the importance/role of volunteers in everyday efforts? In extraordinary times? How has the strata of society shifted, with much more of the public offering more time and resources, in times of intense struggle, and what has this historically meant for nations, economically/socially?

    What is the nature of patriotism? When has there been great patriotic feeling in modern America, and what was the socioeconomic climate at that time? When has there been a lack of patriotic feeling, and what was going on in American history at that time? Does volunteerism also rise and fall accordingly? Is it possible to predict trends in patriotism and volunteerism, based on other societal factors? Why or why not? What does this mean to the historian?

5. We now know that the terrorists who plotted and enacted the September 11, 2001 attacks used email, the Internet and other highly traceable means of technology to communicate with each other. Historically, have societies kept or surrendered their individual rights in the name of safety? Or were they not given that chance? Give examples. What do you think America should do, in terms of keeping or giving up personal freedoms, in the name of safety?

6. Ask the students: Do you agree with the author's notion of generational personality (i.e. the idea that each generation has its own unique characteristic, such as the Baby Boomers' idealism, or Generation X's lack of direction in life)? What are your generation's shared media experiences? In your opinion, what will be the defining moment of your generation, and how will that moment be realized, in terms of a generational personality? (In other words, what will your generation become best known for?) Do you agree with the author's vision of a "Freedom Generation"? Why or why not? What are your solutions for the new challenges we face in world security issues?

Assessment:

Student understanding should be assessed through:

- Contributions to class discussion

- Demonstrated understanding of the events of September 11 (its chronology and grasp of its motivating factors)

- Essay: How has technology influenced the way we wage war and the way we secure peace? OR: What is the history of volunteerism in America? Give four examples of how volunteer efforts have significantly shaped American culture, economy or popular culture in times of conflict.

- Outside research project: In order to show the long memory of the thought behind Jihad resentment toward American culture, and the many influences and sometimes disparate events that led to it, students should create a Jihad Timeline, marking events and phenomena leading to the terrorist mindset. (This may be represented in an actual line, pie graph, or chart, to best suit the student's argument) This will be accompanied by a brief presentation, explaining the history behind Jihad culture and thought, and its relevance to the September 11 attacks.

Lessons Learned at Ground Zero: Lesson Plans for the History Instructor

Grade Level: High School Level
Estimated Time: Three 45-minute sessions, or three class periods

Lesson Overview:

The attack on America on September 11, 2001 was a defining moment in American history. This lesson plan poses important questions that all historians and history students must ask in this post-9/11 era, as we all work to place the Attack on America, and subsequent events, in context with the past.

Materials:

- *Lessons Learned at Ground Zero*

- Access to further research materials (Internet, library) for at-home writing assignments

Procedure:

1. Ask the students: Do you agree with the author's notion of generational personality (i.e. the idea that each generation has its own unique characteristic, such as the Baby Boomers' idealism, or Generation X's lack of direction in life)? Name examples in history to back your opinion. What memories do all people in your generation share in common? In your opinion, what will be the defining moment of your generation? What "personality"—if you do, indeed, agree with that concept—will your generation become best known for? Do you think you will become the "Freedom Generation" as outlined in the text? Why or why not?

    Ask students to think of examples in history when volunteers have stepped in and helped fill important roles in American history. When has patriotism been at its lowest, and highest in modern

American history (give examples)? Why? Is it possible to predict trends in volunteer efforts and patriotism, based on other factors?

2. The attack on America on September 11, 2001 was a defining moment in modern American history. Ask students to share what they know about the event. What historical significance, if any, did the terrorists attach to the September 11 date, and why? Why did the terrorists choose the World Trade Center—and, for that matter, America—as their target?

Does political/cultural/religious climate play a part in a nation's reaction to major events? If so, how?

3. We now know that the terrorists who plotted and enacted the September 11, 2001 attacks used email, the Internet and other highly traceable means of technology to communicate with each other. As a result, we all face a lot of questions regarding the technological invasion of our privacies, versus the safety of ourselves, and our loved ones. Historically, have societies kept or surrendered their individual rights in the name of safety? Or were they not given that chance? What do you think America should do, in terms of keeping or giving up personal freedoms, in the name of safety?

How has technology changed the way we wage war, and the way we make peace? How has it impacted intelligence-gathering? What is the best solution to fighting terrorism today, now that we have so many technological challenges…. And so many technological means of tracking down potential enemies? What are the pitfalls of those technologies? What are its "selling points"?

Assessment:

Student understanding should be assessed through:

a. Contributions to class discussion

b. Demonstrated understanding of the events of September 11 (its chronology and grasp of its motivating factors)

c. Essay: How has technology influenced the way we wage war and the way we secure peace?

d. Outside research project: In order to show the long memory of the thought behind Jihad resentment toward American culture, and the many influences and sometimes disparate events that led to it, students should create a Jihad Timeline, marking events and phenomena leading to the terrorist mindset. (This may be represented in an actual line, pie graph, or chart, to best suit the student's argument) This will be accompanied by a brief presentation, explaining the history behind Jihad culture and thought, and its relevance to the September 11 attack.

Lessons Learned at Ground Zero:
Lesson Plans for the History Instructor

Grade Level: Middle School Level
Estimated Time: Four class periods

Lesson Overview:

The attack on America on September 11, 2001 was a defining moment in American history, and also an important event in all of our lives. This includes the lives, of course, of all of our nation's children, who, like the rest of us, are working to put these events in perspective. The middle school history instructor can help, by framing these events in the context of history, and encouraging thoughtful discussion, using the lesson plans sketched out below.

Materials:

• *Lessons Learned at Ground Zero*

Procedure:

1. Assignment: Read *Lessons Learned at Ground Zero*. (Take home to finish)

2. Ask the students: Do you agree with the author's notion of generational personality (i.e. the idea that each generation has its own unique characteristic, such as the Baby Boomers' idealism, or Generation X's lack of direction in life)? Name examples in history to back your opinion. Do you agree that the author believes all of today's students have negative "shared media memories"?

    What memories do all people in your generation share in common? In your opinion, what will be the defining moment of your generation? What "personality" will your generation become best known for? (if you agree with that concept) Do you think you will become the "Freedom Generation" as outlined in the text? Why or why not?

3. Ask students to think of examples in history when volunteers have stepped in and helped fill important roles in American history. When has patriotism been at its lowest, and highest in modern American history (give examples)? Why? Is it possible to predict trends in volunteer efforts and patriotism, based on other factors?

4. Ask students to share what they know about the September 11, 2001 event. Who are the Jihad, and what do they believe? Do all Afghani people believe the same? What historical significance, if any, did the terrorists attach to the September 11 date, and why? Why did the terrorists choose the World Trade Center—and, for that matter, America—as their target?

Refer to Part III of *Lessons Learned at Ground Zero*, when the author discusses ways in which other generations have faced extreme situations throughout history. How did they cope? What can we learn from history, to lead us into the future? Give examples.

Assessment:

Student understanding should be assessed through:

a. Contributions to class discussion

b. Demonstrated understanding of the events of September 11 (its chronology and grasp of its motivating factors)

c. Personal essay: What is the best solution for peace?

d. Outside research project: In order to show the long memory of the thought behind Jihad resentment toward American culture, and the many influences and sometimes disparate events that led to it, students should create a Jihad Timeline, marking events and phenomena leading to the terrorist mindset. (This may be represented in an actual line, pie graph, or chart, to best suit the student's argument) This will be accompanied by a brief presentation, explaining the history behind Jihad culture and thought, and its relevance to the September 11 attack.

Lessons Learned at Ground Zero:
Lesson Plans for the Philosophy Instructor

Grade Level: AP High School/University Level
Estimated Time: Six one-hour sessions, or six class periods

Lesson Overview:

How do we qualify the events of September 11, 2001? The media has offered us images and analyses, bringing our questions into a structured arena, and placing them into an informed, inquisitive and scholarly context, the philosophy instructor can shed new light onto this important subject of modern thought.

Materials:

* *Lessons Learned at Ground Zero*

Procedure:

1. The volunteer effort at Ground Zero was enormous. What is the nature and history of volunteerism and patriotism, and what are its effects in society as a whole? Does it impact historical movements? Generational "personality"? If so, how? Why do we feel this need to belong to a group? Is the impulse toward altruism universal? If so, is it learned, or inborn?

2. In the text, the author discusses the reaction of the medical community to his volunteer efforts at Ground Zero. What was that reaction, and how did it differ from that of individuals? What was the reaction of hospitals? Of church groups? Of the officials at the police department? Of the officers themselves? The author also discussed the officers' fears that they would receive "light duty" if they sought counseling. Do the students feel that this system of medical care and medical insurance provision is practical? Is it ethical?

3. What are the views of the Jihad terrorists? Is there such a thing as a holy, "just" war? Why or why not? Is it possible for both sides of a war to be "holy" or "just"? Why or why not? Is there an objective definition for these terms?

    What are the cultural and religious differences between Afghani and American culture that led to the September 22, 2000 attacks? What is the distinction between cultural and religious values? Are the views of the terrorists generally the same views of most of the nation's citizens? If so, should a nation fail to act against another nation because of the actions of a few?

4. Discuss the practice of profiling terrorists. What are the ramifications? Is it an ethical practice, and why or why not? What are possible alternatives?

5. Ask students to discuss the historical conflicts, alliances and cultural/religious differences that led to the Jihad's resentment of American culture, and, ultimately, the attacks of September 11. What is the United States' best approach to peacemaking, given this information? What is the United States' best approach to peacemaking, from an ethical point of view?

    Can individual citizens impact peacemaking efforts between nations, and if so, how? What does the author of *Lessons Learned at Ground Zero* suggest that American citizens do? Do the students agree with his solutions?

6. What is the nature of generational "personality" (discussed in Part III of Lessons Learned at Ground Zero)? Do the students agree with the author's (and popular culture's) notion that generations of people within a nation have distinctive, shared traits? If so, what shapes these traits, and why? Does being a part of a generation of a distinct "personality" form the individual's personality, or vice-versa? What is the "stamp" of this generation, and why? What are

the moral implications of realizing the stamp of one's generation—and wanting to alter it?

Assessment:

Student understanding should be assessed through:

- Contributions to class discussion

- Demonstrated understanding of the events of September 11 (its chronology and basic grasp of motivating factors)

- Class debate: The terrorists believed they were waging a holy war. Is there such a thing as a "just" war? Divide class up into two groups, one pro and one con. Then do the exercise (briefly) again; this time, the two groups will represent: Afghani and American.

- Opinion essay: Terrorist profiling: Ramifications and ethical consequences.

Lessons Learned at Ground Zero:
A Lesson Guide for the Psychology Instructor

Grade Level: AP High School/University Level
Estimated Time: Five one-hour sessions, or five class periods

Lesson Overview:

All across the nation, psychologists and psychology students are asking: "What are the psychological roots of terrorism?" "What are the effects of profiling?" "How do different people respond to catastrophic, terrorist-driven events?" and, ultimately, "How do we treat them, and—as a society—face the prospect of an uncertain future as we heal?" Through these lessons, students will learn about profiling practices, how different individuals react to traumatic situations, Post-Traumatic Stress Disorder and different international agencies working to eliminate terrorism, and will debate the effectiveness of various proposed measures of addressing the terrorist mindset, domestically and worldwide.

Materials:

• *Lessons Learned at Ground Zero*

Procedure:

1. What are the psychological roots of the terrorist events on September 11, 2001 (i.e. why did they feel and act as they did)? *For example, to what extent are cultural factors responsible? To what extent are religious factors responsible? To what extent is it a matter of particular beliefs of the Jihad, and not a reflection of the nation, as a whole? Can the behavior be explained by personal events, and can it be explained by shared defining experiences, such as conflicts with Israel?*

    Can you point to any predictors of terrorist behavior—in individuals, and/or in nations?

2. In *Lessons Learned at Ground Zero*, Dr. Rob Gillio discussed his father's experiences at Iwo Jima in relation to his experiences at Ground Zero, and related his own feelings as an on-site volunteer, as he listened to First Responders discuss their reactions to the events. Encourage students to discuss their own responses during and after the events at the World Trade Center bombing, and ask them to compare/contrast these reactions to the First Responders' reactions during and after the event. How are these emotions/reactions similar to, and different from, those of the on-site volunteers (including the author's)? What were the volunteers' motives? Did you feel that the author's opinions and responses were honest/genuine and appropriate? Why or why not?

   How does Dr. Rob help First Responders, and how might psychologists help First Responders and victims of the attacks deal with such large-scale events as the World Trade Center Bombing? What does Dr. Rob suggest that ordinary citizens do to help prepare for future events? What do the students think is the best approach?

3. While at Ground Zero, Dr. Rob noticed that some of the "cadaver dogs"—rescue dogs used to sniff out corpses at the site of the wreckage—were overstimulated; others were despondent. To buoy their spirits, workers hid in the rubble, so that the dogs would be able to experience finding live humans. Is there room in the "serious" psychological world for the treatment of animal behavior?

   And, if *animal* rescuers experienced this much trauma and depression, what are the effects of such an event on *human* rescuers? What might the psychological profile be of the rescuer/volunteer? What can psychologists do to treat them, when they are traumatized by extreme rescue efforts?

4. Discuss the practice of profiling terrorists. Is it a positive or negative force in society? What might this mean, in terms of the psychologist's role in international affairs? What might this mean, in

terms of the freedoms of American citizens? What suggestions do the students have, to help address domestic terrorism.

5.   Discuss Post-Traumatic Stress Disorder—a diagnosis that began to be recognized after the effects of it were noted in World War II veterans, and gained more public recognition after the return of the Vietnam War soldiers to American soil. What are its symptoms? Why do PTSD and clinical depression afflict some victims of a short-term event (such as a bombing), as well as a long-term event (such as a tour of duty), and not others?

What role does increased adrenaline and chemical imbalance play in human behavior overall? Cite examples.

Assessment:

Student understanding should be assessed through:

a.   Contributions to class discussion

b.   Demonstrated understanding of the events of September 11 (its chronology and basic grasp of motivating factors)

c.   Written definition of Post-Traumatic Stress Disorder, and list symptoms. Why do PTSD and clinical depression affect some victims of traumatic events—and their rescuers, as well as onlookers—and not others?

d.   Written definition of the practice of profiling; discuss pros and cons. Discuss the psychologist's role in combating domestic terrorism.

e.   List of the five recommendations for combating terrorism, with explanations for each

f.   Research the terrorist profile. Why did the terrorists behave as they did? Write an opinion essay on the terrorist mindset and list possible recommendations for peacemaking.

Lessons Learned at Ground Zero: Lesson Plans for the Science Instructor

Grade Level: University level
Estimated Time: Three 45-minute sessions, or three class periods

Lesson Overview:

Lessons Learned at Ground Zero is a book that chronicles a doctor's experiences while volunteering to help test First Responders who worked at the site of the World Trade Center, following the attacks of September 11, 2001. A pulmonary expert and practicing doctor for more than 20 years, the author recounts his personal experiences at Ground Zero as he explains the possible dangers that airborne contaminants—sent into the air by a large-impact bombing or accident of this nature—can cause, and the inventions he created and modified for on-site diagnosis and disaster response. These questions will help address questions that scientists ask in the post-9/11 era, as sparked by the *Lessons Learned at Ground Zero* text.

Materials:

• *Lessons Learned at Ground Zero*

Procedure:

1. What contaminants did the author, Dr. Rob Gillio, find at Ground Zero, and how were they caused? What was his greatest concern for First Responders' health, and why? What can the scientist and doctor do to address these concerns for these workers, and for future attacks?

2. Discuss the use of technology for diagnostic and emergency response purposes at Ground Zero: What are the pros and cons of such peacetime/wartime dual-response machinery? What other

inventions can you think of to help make the cleanup of disaster sites easier and safer?

3. What role does the chemist/scientist play in combating terrorism? How did you see this in action in *Lessons Learned at Ground Zero*? How can you use what you have learned thus far in this class and apply it to homeland security issues? In this regard, what is the role of the biologist and chemist in the post-9/11 America?

Assessment:

Student understanding should be assessed through:

- Contributions to class discussion. Understanding of effect of contaminants on the environment and on pulmonary health.

- Essay: The Scientist and Homeland Security: What is the role of the Scientist in the future?

Lessons Learned at Ground Zero:
Lesson Plans for the Social Studies Instructor

Grade Level: High School Level
Estimated Time: Three one-hour sessions, or three class periods

Lesson Overview:

These lesson plans pose important questions that all sociologists must ask in this post-9/11 era, namely: "What effects do monumental events such as these have on societies, as a whole?" "What is the terrorist profile, and what are the roots of terrorism?" "What are the effects of profiling?", "How do different individuals and peoples respond to catastrophic, terrorist-driven events?" "Is there such a thing as a 'generational personality' and if so, how is it impacted by shared monumental events?" and, ultimately, "How do we, as a society, deal the prospect of an uncertain future as we work to heal?"

Materials:

* *Lessons Learned at Ground Zero*

Procedure:

1. What are the cultural and religious differences between Afghani and American culture that led to the September 22, 2000 attacks? What is the distinction between cultural and religious values? Are the views of the terrorists generally the same views of most of the nation's citizens? If so, should a nation fail to act against another nation because of the actions of a few?

2. Discuss racial profiling. Is it a good thing, or a bad thing, and why? What are possible alternatives to locating and stopping the actions of potential and present terrorists?

3. Ask students to discuss the historical conflicts, alliances and cultural/religious differences that led to the Jihad's resentment of American culture, and, ultimately, the attacks of September 11. What is the United States' best approach to peacemaking, given the current socioeconomic climate, and given these factors?

Assessment:

Student understanding should be assessed through:

- Contributions to class discussion

- Demonstrated understanding of the events of September 11 (its chronology and basic grasp of motivating factors)

- Define practice of profiling; discuss pros and cons.

- List five recommendations for combating terrorism, with explanations for each.

- Research the terrorist profile, and write an opinion paper: Why did the terrorists act as they did, and what are your recommendations for the United States' response?

Lessons Learned at Ground Zero:
Lesson Plans for the Sociology Instructor

Grade Level: University Level
Estimated Time: Four one-hour sessions, or four class periods

Lesson Overview:

These lesson plans pose important questions that all sociologists must ask in this post-9/11 era, namely: "What effects do monumental events such as these have on societies, as a whole?" "What is the terrorist profile, and what are the roots of terrorism?" "What are the effects of profiling?" "How do different individuals and peoples respond to catastrophic, terrorist-driven events?" "Is there such a thing as a 'generational personality' and if so, how is it impacted by shared monumental events?" and, ultimately, "How do we, as a society, deal with the prospect of an uncertain future as we work to heal?"

Materials:

• *Lessons Learned at Ground Zero*

Procedure:

1. The attack on America on September 11, 2001 constituted a seminal moment in modern American history. Ask students to share what they know about the event, and why the terrorists chose the World Trade Center—and, for that matter, America—as their target. Why did they use commercial airlines?

   What are some of the *cultural* differences that led to the terrorists' views of Americans? (Is there a distinction between cultural and religious values? If so, explain.) Are the views of the terrorists generally the same views of most of the nation's citizens? What does the author, Dr. Rob Gillio, suggest that American citizens do, on an interpersonal level, to combat the terrorist movement? Do the students agree with his solutions? Why or why not?

2. In *Lessons Learned at Ground Zero*, Dr. Rob discussed his father's experiences at Iwo Jima in relation to his experiences at Ground Zero, and related his own feelings as an on-site volunteer, as he listened to First Responders discuss their reactions to the events. Ask students to relate other instances of terrorism and shared traumatic experience in modern history.

    Are any of these experiences as wide-reaching as the events of September 11? Are any high-impact events continuing today? What are the effects of these events on rescuers, on victims, on active participants in the conflict, on "people back home"? Does reaction vary throughout history, and from culture to culture? Does political/cultural/religious climate play a part, and if so, how?

3. Discuss the generational attributes, or generational "personalities" that Dr. Rob outlines briefly in Part 3 of the text (i.e. the Baby Boomer Generation vs. the "Me" Generation, vs. Generation X vs. Generation Y). Do the students believe that each generation has a distinct personality, or "stamp," marked by its times? If so, what do they believe will be the marker of their own generation? Do they believe it will affect the "personality" of their generation (such as in Dr. Rob's proposal that this generation become the "Freedom" Generation)? What do the students think are some of the markers (if any) of this generation of Afghani citizens?

    Can a generation of citizens influence peacemaking (or war-making) efforts between nations?

4. Discuss the practice of profiling terrorists. Is profiling ultimately a positive or negative practice? What might this mean, in terms of the freedoms of American citizens? What suggestions do the students have, to help combat domestic terrorism? What does this mean, in terms of international intelligence-gathering?

Assessment:

Student understanding should be assessed through:

- Contributions to class discussion

- Demonstrated understanding of the events of September 11 (its chronology and basic grasp of motivating factors)

- Opinion essay: What is the defining moment of your generation? Do you think your generation will indeed become known as the "Freedom Generation," as suggested in the text? For what attributes or works do you believe your generation will be known?

- Students will break up into three groups, of even numbers: "pro," "con" and "jury". A class debate about the pros and cons of terrorist profiling will ensue. The "jury" will award one point to each member of the pertinent group for each salient (non-repetitive) point made. This would be graded under the category of class participation.

- Research the terrorist profile, and write an essay outlining the similarities and differences between Afghani and American cultures. Or: Write an opinion essay on the terrorist mindset and list possible recommendations for peacemaking.

PART THREE: TOOLS FOR MOTIVATION AND TRAINING IN THE COMMUNITY

PREPARE YOUR COMMUNITY:
A Guide for Schools, Churches, Scouting Groups, Block Watch Groups, CERTS, and Other Community Organizations

Since all emergencies are initially handled locally, it is imperative that the community be ready to respond. As stated within the text of the book, the better a sense of cohesion and organization within the community during peacetime, the more smoothly events will operate, should extraordinary events occur. All citizens must be included in the preparation of homeland security. Improving the status of everyone in the community will alleviate the risks of overtaxing the resources of the community during the emergency. Past events have shown that if groups work to attain a true sense of cohesion, equality and community during peacetime, this will help prevent looting and other social breakdown if a disaster strikes.

In more practical terms, the better prepared your community is (in terms of medicine stockpiles, power generation, food supply and so on), the less likely your community will be to find itself in an extreme situation, when desperate people do desperate things in order to survive. The best way to accomplish optimal preparation is for citizens to pool their resources, working together in ordinary times, so that they are ready for the extraordinary.

The time to be prepared for the unexpected, then, is now. How do you know whether or not your community is well-prepared for an extraordinary event?

Ask your officials:

- Is there a disaster plan in place?

- Is there a community web site for up-to-date information and directions for the citizens or volunteers?

- Has this plan been updated since the onset of bioterrorism in this country, and since the airplane has been used a weapon of mass destruction against us?

- Is this plan available to your SWAT team, police, fire and rescue worker?

- Is there a database of volunteers, including their skills?

- Are there secure communications with secondary authorities to get advice and referral for additional assistance?

- Can your police radios talk to your fire department or ambulance workers?

- Are there evacuation routes?

- Are your fire companies on the verge of bankruptcy and using outmoded equipment?

- Are the schools equipped and prepared to act as community centers or field hospitals?

- Are there sufficient supplies for the police, fire, water, electrical and sanitation workers to perform safely and adequately?

- I am aware of officers who purchase their own guns and radios to be sure they will work, but do your civil servants have baseline screening evaluations of lung function and electrocardiograms in an accessible medical record?

Consider creating a Community Preparedness Event with a screening health fair combined with training and information on these issues, which can be used to start a database of skills, resources, and volunteers available in an emergency.

Are your own professional associations or organizations preparing a list of resources and actions in the event of a disaster? Are there disaster plan web sites and manuals available for your school, office and community? Is there Community Preparedness Council or other Freedom Corps activity active in your community?

About the Author

Dr. Robert Gillio is a 47-year-old father of four daughters who attend elementary and high schools. He is a Board Certified pulmonologist who trained for six years at the Mayo Clinic and then operated a successful practice treating critically ill patients suffering from asthma, emphysema and lung cancer. He was the first winner of the prestigious Doctor of the Year award at his hospital and loves the practice of medicine.

He also loves to solve problems. He is a recognized inventor and innovator in the fields of medication dispensing, surgical simulation, telemedicine, Internet education and case-based simulation. He has been awarded thirteen patents and has assembled teams to create companies that can take his ideas into distribution to solve problems.

To spend more time with his daughters, and to engage them and other students in the excitement of creativity, scientific exploration and working with real experts on problem solving, he gave up his successful practice and founded InnerLink, Inc. He recruited talented management and staff to involve students in world-class projects.

These have included work on the International Space Station and a second project geared to dissuade young people from beginning to smoke, or to quit if they already have begun. The anti-smoking project includes research on inhalation injuries, exploring the use of telemedicine equipment for use in school science classes and applying a community lung screening program in a career education curriculum.

About the Editors

MaryAlice Bitts

MaryAlice Bitts is a book editor, a magazine editor, a public relations specialist, an online news content editor and a freelance writer journalist specializing in arts criticism/education/review and educational journals. Her art, music, theater and travel reviews, feature articles, edited text and poetry have appeared in many publications, and she has earned seven Women in Communications Awards for excellence in journalism and editing. Her skills also include web design, small group instruction and grant writing.

Ms. Bitts earned a bachelors of arts in English and a BA in music from Marywood College. She is currently pursuing multiple Master's degrees from the Pennsylvania State University in humanities (interdisciplinary fine arts), psychology and education, with an emphasis on writing. She enjoys writing music, painting, designing jewelry, tutoring, reading and traveling, having studied in Australia and Europe, and taken medical supplies to Russia. She also designed the logo on the cover of this book.

Chance Conner

Chance Conner is a screenwriter, speechwriter, and journalist with a broad knowledge of news, politics business and sports. Having earned his bachelor's degree in journalism at the Pennsylvania State University, Chance was a Fellow of both the Knight Center for Specialized Journalism (University of Maryland, College Park, 1995) and the German Press Seminar (Berlin and Bonn, 1993, studying the reunification of Germany). In September 1991 he became the *Denver Post*'s lead reporter on the Oklahoma City's bombing case—an assignment that earned him the Colorado Press Association's award for Best Continuous News Coverage, 1997.

A politically active person, Mr. Conner has worked as press secretary for the Henry Strauss for Congress campaign and communications director for the Dave Thomas for U.S. Congress campaign.

0-595-24350-9

Printed in the United States
55574LVS00005B/1-102

9 780595 243501